Real

Listening & Speaking 3
with answers

Miles Craven

CAMBRIDGE
UNIVERSITY PRESS

CAMBRIDGE UNIVERSITY PRESS
Cambridge, New York, Melbourne, Madrid, Cape Town,
Singapore, São Paulo, Delhi, Mexico City

Cambridge University Press
The Edinburgh Building, Cambridge CB2 8RU, UK

www.cambridge.org
Information on this title: www.cambridge.org/9780521705882

First published 2008
9th printing 2013

Printed in Poland by Opolgraf

A catalogue record for this publication is available from the British Library

ISBN 978-0-521-70588-2 Paperback

Contents

Map of the book

Work and Study

The author would like to thank all the Cambridge University Press team involved in the development of *Real Listening and Speaking 3* for their commitment, enthusiasm and outstanding support, especially Nóirín Burke, Roslyn Henderson, Caroline Thiriau, Linda Matthews and Martine Walsh. Very special thanks also to Hilary Ratcliff for her excellent editing, to Stephanie White and Paul Fellows for their design expertise, and to Bell International for the use of their wonderful facilities. Finally, I would like to thank Jessica for her love, patience and support, which makes all things possible.

The author and publishers are grateful to the following reviewers for their valuable insights and suggestions:

Kathryn Alevizos, UK
Steve Banfield, UAE
Nigel Daly, Taiwan
Rosie Ganne, UK
Rui da Silva, UK
Helen Dixon, UK
Barbara Gardner, UK
Hebe Gomez, Spain
Peter Gray, Japan
Jean Greenwood, UK
Beatriz Martin, Spain
Dr Zbigniew Mozejko, Poland
Paul Seligson, UK
Raymond Sheehan, UAE.

The authors and publishers would like to thank the following for permission to reproduce photographs:

Key: l = left, c = centre, r = right, t = top, b = bottom

Alamy/©Image Shop for p. 21 (r) /©Spotlight Software & Photography Ltd for p. 38 /©Ian Shaw for p. 75; Corbis Images/©Kristy-Anne Glubish/Design Pics for p. 28 /©Helen King for p. 56; Eye Ubiquitous/©Hutchison/Mel Longhurst for p. 40; Getty Images for p. 11; Photolibrary/©Image 100 for p. 18; Punchstock/©fancy for p. 17 /©Image Source for p. 19 /©Glowimages for p. 21 (l) /©Stockbyte for p. 24 /©Bananastock for p. 32 /©Image Source for p. 35 /©Brand X for p. 61; Shutterstock/©Yegor Korzh for p. 27; Still Pictures/©Nick Cobbing/Greenpeace for p. 66.

Illustrations:

Kathy Baxendale pp. 30, 53b; Mark Duffin pp. 13, 18, 36, 39, 48t, 56, 68t; Kamae Design p. 55; Katie Mac pp. 10, 22, 34, 46, 64; Laura Martinez pp. 14, 26, 48b, 54, 65, 68b; Julian Mosedale pp. 44; Ian West pp. 32, 53t, 72.

Text design and page make-up: Kamae Design, Oxford
Cover design: Kamae Design, Oxford
Cover photo: © Getty Images
Picture research: Hilary Luckcock

Introduction
To the student

Who is *Real Listening & Speaking 3* for?

You can use this book if you are a student at intermediate – upper intermediate level and you want to improve your English listening and speaking. You can use the book alone without a teacher or you can use it in a classroom with a teacher.

How will *Real Listening & Speaking 3* help me with my listening and speaking?

Real Listening and Speaking 3 contains practical tasks to help you in everyday listening and speaking situations, e.g. at the shops, in a restaurant or travelling away from home. It also gives practice in a range of work and study situations. It is designed to help you with listening and speaking tasks you will need to do when communicating in English, at home or abroad.

The exercises in each unit help you to develop useful skills, such as listening for opinions, listening for details and listening for the main idea. There are also lots of practical speaking strategies and tasks that help you improve your ability to communicate, and pronunciation activities too.

How is *Real Listening and Speaking 3* organized?

The book has 16 units and is divided into two main sections:
- Units 1–8 – social or travel situations
- Units 9–16 – work or study situations

Every unit has:
- *Get ready to listen and speak*: introduces you to the topic of the unit
- *Learning tip*: helps you improve your learning
- *Class bonus*: gives an exercise that you can do with other students or friends
- *Speaking strategy*: explains a useful strategy
- *Speak up!*: practises the strategy
- *Extra practice*: gives an extra exercise for more practice
- *Can-do checklist*: helps you think about what you learnt in the unit

Most units also have:
- *Focus on*: helps you study useful grammar or vocabulary
- *Did you know?*: gives extra information about vocabulary, different cultures or the topic of the unit
- *Sound smart*: helps you with pronunciation

After each main section, there is a review unit. The reviews help you to practise the skills you learn in each section.

At the back of the book you can find:
- *Appendices*: contain lists of *Useful language*, Pronunciation features and Speaking strategies, as well as a Presentation evaluation to complete.
- *Audioscript*: includes everything that you can hear on the audio CD and gives information about the nationalities of the speakers
- *Answer key*: gives correct answers and possible answers for exercises that have more than one answer

How can I use *Real Listening & Speaking 3*?

The book is in two sections: *Social and Travel*, and *Work and Study*. The units at the end of the book are more difficult than the units at the beginning of the book. However, you do not need to do the units in order. It is better to choose the units that are most interesting for you and to do them in the order you prefer.

There are many different ways you can use this book. We suggest you work in this way:
- Look in the *Contents* list and find a unit that interests you.
- Go to *Appendix 1* and look at the *Useful language* for the unit you want to do. You can use a dictionary to help you understand the words and expressions.
- Do the *Get ready to listen and speak* section at the start of the unit. This will introduce you to the topic of the unit.
- Do the other exercises in the unit. At the end of each exercise, check your answers in the *Answer key*.
- If your answers are wrong, study the section again to see where you made mistakes.
- Try to do the listening exercises without looking at the audioscript. You can read the audioscript after you finish the exercises.
- If you want to do more work in this unit, do the *Extra practice* activity.
- At the end of the unit, think about what you learnt and complete the *Can-do checklist*.
- Go to *Appendix 1* and look at the *Useful language* for the unit again.

What is *Cambridge English Skills*?

Real Listening & Speaking 3 is one of 12 books in the *Cambridge English Skills* series. The series also contains *Real Reading* and *Real Writing* books and offers skills training to students from elementary to advanced level. All the books are available in with-answers and without-answers editions.

Level	Book	Author
Elementary CEF: A2 Cambridge ESOL: KET NQF Skills for life: Entry 2	Real Reading 1 with answers	Liz Driscoll
	Real Reading 1 without answers	Liz Driscoll
	Real Writing 1 with answers and audio CD	Graham Palmer
	Real Writing 1 without answers	Graham Palmer
	Real Listening & Speaking 1 with answers and audio CDs (2)	Miles Craven
	Real Listening & Speaking 1 without answers	Miles Craven
Pre-intermediate CEF: B1 Cambridge ESOL: PET NQF Skills for life: Entry 3	Real Reading 2 with answers	Liz Driscoll
	Real Reading 2 without answers	Liz Driscoll
	Real Writing 2 with answers and audio CD	Graham Palmer
	Real Writing 2 without answers	Graham Palmer
	Real Listening & Speaking 2 with answers and audio CDs (2)	Sally Logan & Craig Thaine
	Real Listening & Speaking 2 without answers	Sally Logan & Craig Thaine
Intermediate to upper-intermediate CEF: B2 Cambridge ESOL: FCE NQF Skills for life: Level 1	Real Reading 3 with answers	Liz Driscoll
	Real Reading 3 without answers	Liz Driscoll
	Real Writing 3 with answers and audio CD	Roger Gower
	Real Writing 3 without answers	Roger Gower
	Real Listening & Speaking 3 with answers and audio CDs (2)	Miles Craven
	Real Listening & Speaking 3 without answers	Miles Craven
Advanced CEF: C1 Cambridge ESOL: CAE NQF Skills for life: Level 2	Real Reading 4 with answers	Liz Driscoll
	Real Reading 4 without answers	Liz Driscoll
	Real Writing 4 with answers and audio CD	Simon Haines
	Real Writing 4 without answers	Simon Haines
	Real Listening & Speaking 4 with answers and audio CDs (2)	Miles Craven
	Real Listening & Speaking 4 without answers	Miles Craven

Where are the teacher's notes?

The series is accompanied by a dedicated website containing detailed teaching notes and extension ideas for every unit of every book. Please visit www.cambridge.org/englishskills to access the *Cambridge English Skills* teacher's notes.

What are the main aims of *Real Listening & Speaking 3*?

- To help students develop listening and speaking skills in accordance with the ALTE (Association of Language Testers in Europe) can-do statements. These statements describe what language users can typically do at different levels and in different contexts. Visit www.alte.org for further information.
- To encourage autonomous learning by focusing on learner training

What are the key features of *Real Listening & Speaking 3*?

- It is aimed at intermediate and upper intermediate learners of English at levels B1–B2 of the Council of Europe's CEFR (Common European Framework of Reference for Languages).
- It contains 16 four-page units, divided into two sections: Social and Travel, and Work and Study.
- *Real Listening & Speaking 3* units contain:
  - *Get ready to listen and speak* warm-up tasks to get students thinking about the topic
  - *Learning tip* boxes which give students advice on how to improve their listening and speaking and their learning
  - *Focus on* activities which provide contextualized practice in particular language or vocabulary areas
  - *Class bonus* communication activities for pairwork and group work so you can adapt the material to suit your class
  - *Did you know?* boxes which provide notes on cultural or linguistic differences between English-speaking countries, or factual information on the topic of the unit
  - *Extra practice* extension tasks which provide more real-world listening and speaking practice
  - *Can-do checklist* at the end of every unit to encourage students to think about what they have learnt.
- There are two review units to practise skills that have been introduced in the units.
- It covers a wide range of highly practical activities that give students the skills they need to communicate effectively in everyday situations.
- It has an international feel and contains a range of native and non-native accents.
- It can be used as self-study material, in class, or as supplementary homework material.

What is the best way to use *Real Listening & Speaking 3* in the classroom?

The book is designed so that there is no set way to work through the units. The units may be used in any order, although the more difficult units naturally appear near the end of the book, in the Work and Study section.

You can consult the unit-by-unit teacher's notes at www.cambridge.org/englishskills for detailed teaching ideas. However, as a general guide, different sections of the book can be approached in the following ways:

- *Useful language*: Use the *Useful language* lists in the *Appendices* to preteach or revise the vocabulary from the unit you are working on.
- *Get ready to listen and speak*: It's a good idea to use this section as an introduction to the topic. Students can work on these exercises in pairs or groups. Some exercises require students to answer questions about their personal experience. These questions can be used as prompts for discussion. Some exercises contain a problem-solving element that students can work on together. Other exercises aim to clarify key vocabulary in the unit. You can present these vocabulary items directly to students.
- *Learning tips*: Focus on these and draw attention to them in an open class situation. An alternative approach is for you to create a series of discussion questions associated with the *Learning tip*. Students can discuss their ideas in pairs or small groups, followed by open class feedback. The *Learning tip* acts as a reflective learning tool to help promote learner autonomy.
- *Class bonuses*: The material in these activities aims to provide freer practice. You can set these up carefully, and then take the role of observer during the activity so that students carry out the task freely. You can make yourself available to help students to analyze the language they produce during the activity.
- *Extra practice*: These tasks can be set as homework or out-of-class projects for your students. Students can do some tasks in pairs during class time.
- *Can-do checklists*: Refer to these at the beginning of a lesson to explain to students what the lesson will cover, and again at the end so that students can evaluate their learning for themselves.
- *Audioscript*: Occasionally non-native speaker spoken errors are included in the audio material. They are labelled *Did you notice?* in the audioscript and can be used in the classroom to focus on common errors.

Unit 1
How are things?

Get ready to **listen and speak**

- For each expression, write 1 (to start a conversation), 2 (to try to end a conversation), 3 (to say goodbye).

Hi there. ☐1   How are you doing? ☐   Talk to you later. ☐

I've got to go. ☐2   See you around. ☐   I guess I'd better be going. ☐

See you later. ☐3   Have a nice weekend. ☐   Right, I must dash. ☐

How's it going? ☐   What's up? ☐   It was nice talking with you. ☐

go to Useful language p. 78

A Listening – Beginning and ending a conversation

1 🔊2 **Listen and match each conversation (1–4) with a picture (a–d).**

a

☐

b

☐

c

☐

d

☐1

2 🔊2 **Listen to each conversation again. Tick ✓ the expressions in** *Get ready to listen and speak* **that you hear.**

3 🔊2 **Listen once more and add any more expressions to the list.**

B Listening – A friendly chat

1 ⬤13 **Martin and Ana work together in Singapore. Listen and answer the questions.**

  a Do they know each other? ....

  b Where do you think they work? ....

2 ⬤13 **Listen again and tick ✓ True, False or Don't know.**

	True	False	Don't know
a Ana started her job a month ago.	☐	✓	☐
b She works on reception.	☐	☐	☐
c She is from Brazil.	☐	☐	☐
d Martin hasn't been in Singapore long.	☐	☐	☐
e He has had the same job for three years.	☐	☐	☐
f Ana used to work in London.	☐	☐	☐
g Many of her family live in London.	☐	☐	☐
h She left her last job because of stress.	☐	☐	☐

Did you know …?

Singapore has four official languages: Malay, Mandarin Chinese, Tamil and English. Many people also speak 'Singlish', a Singaporean version of English.

C Speaking – Reacting to what you hear

Speaking strategy: Agreeing

1 **You can be friendly by saying *Me too* or *Me neither* to agree with the person you are speaking to. This also shows you have understood and helps to keep the conversation going. Look at these extracts from Martin and Ana's conversation.**

Ana: How long have you been here in Singapore?

Martin: Nearly three years now. I like it a lot.

Ana: *Me too.*

Ana: I don't like big cities.

Martin: *Me neither.*

Speak up!

2 ⬤14 **Listen to each statement and agree using *Me too* or *Me neither*.**

Example: a
You hear: I don't like chicken.
You say: Me neither.

Focus on …
So … I, Neither … I

ab **C** def 🔍

You can say *So … I* and *Neither … I* to agree with someone. Read the statements and complete each response using a word below.

will   did   would   do   can   am   could   have   ~~do~~   had

a I like fish and chips.   So ___*do*___ I.

b I don't usually go to parties.   Neither _____ I.

c I can't wait for the weekend.   Neither _____ I.

d I'm going to the cinema tonight.   So _____ I.

e I won't go to the party tomorrow.   Neither _____ I.

f I've been to Africa, you know.   So _____ I.

g I watched the football last night.   So _____ I.

h I'd never eaten snails.   Neither _____ I.

i I couldn't swim when I was young.   Neither _____ I.

j I'd like to go shopping tomorrow.   So _____ I.

D Speaking – Maintaining a conversation

Speaking strategy: Asking follow-up questions

1 Look at this extract from the conversation between Martin and Ana. Notice the follow-up question that Martin asks.

Martin: Where were you before you moved here?
Ana: At the Regent Palace, in London.
Martin: *That's a big place, isn't it?*

2 Think of at least two possible follow-up questions for each statement below.

a I went to the cinema last night.
   What did you see? Who did you go with?

b I work in New York.

c My computer doesn't work.

d I bought a jumper yesterday.

e I'm going to start a cookery course soon.

Speak up!

3 ◆5 Listen to five statements. Respond with follow-up questions.

Example: a
You hear: I read a book at the weekend, but it was terrible.
You say: Oh, really? What book did you read? / Why didn't you like it?

Learning tip

When you are talking with someone, you should try to participate as actively as you can. As well as reacting to what you hear, you should develop the conversation further by asking additional questions to find out more information.

Class bonus

1 Imagine you and your partner were on holiday last week. Write five statements about what you did on your holiday.
2 Find a new partner and take turns to talk about your holiday. How many follow-up questions can your partner ask about each statement?

Sound smart
Intonation in question tags

1 ◆6 The way you say a question tag gives its meaning. Listen to the same sentence spoken twice. In A the speaker is asking a genuine question, but in B the speaker is asking for agreement.

A Helen lives in Hong Kong, doesn't she?
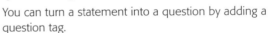

B Helen lives in Hong Kong, doesn't she?

2 Circle the correct answer to complete the rules.
To ask a genuine question, your voice should go UP / DOWN.
To ask for agreement, your voice should go UP / DOWN.

3 ◆7 Listen to these sentences and tick ✓ the ones that are genuine questions.
a ✓   b ☐   c ☐   d ☐   e ☐
f ☐   g ☐   h ☐   i ☐   j ☐

4 ◆7 Listen again and repeat each sentence using the same intonation.

Focus on ...
question tags

You can turn a statement into a question by adding a question tag.
We add a negative question tag to a positive statement:
That was a great movie, wasn't it?
We add a positive question tag to a negative statement:
You didn't see Miki, did you?

Turn each statement into a question by adding a question tag.

isn't she   don't you   ~~aren't they~~   should we
have you   would you   won't we   won't they
did you   do you   have you   wasn't it

a Those are my car keys, _____aren't they_____ ?
b Lisa is a police officer, _____ ?
c You didn't say that, _____ ?
d You know I'm right, _____ ?
e We'll always be friends, _____ ?
f You don't know the answer, _____ ?
g You wouldn't leave me alone here, _____ ?
h We shouldn't be here, _____ ?
i You haven't seen this film before, _____ ?
j They will be here on time, _____ ?
k You haven't got a brother, _____ ?
l That lecture was a bit boring, _____ ?

E Listening – Expressing opinions

1 🔘 **1.8** Listen and match each conversation (1–6) with a topic (a–f).

2 🔘 **1.8** Listen to each conversation again. Do the people agree or disagree?

1 Agree

2 _____

3 _____

4 _____

5 _____

6 _____

3 🔘 **1.8** Listen once more and write three expressions in each column.

a smoking ☐

b exams 1

c computer games ☐

d vegetarianism ☐

e traffic ☐

f obesity ☐

Expressions to agree with someone	Expressions to disagree with someone
That's exactly what I think.	

F Speaking – Defending opinions

Speaking strategy: Arguing your point

1 Match each statement (a–e) with a response (1–5).

a I think politicians these days are all the same. 4

b I believe that marriage should be for life. ☐

c From my point of view, killing animals for sport is wrong. ☐

d It seems to me that the world is getting more dangerous. ☐

e In my opinion, working overtime is too stressful. ☐

1 **You may be right, but** a lot of people enjoy hunting.

2 **I may be wrong, but** isn't there less crime these days?

3 **I agree to some extent, but** the extra money is handy.

4 **Yes, but** it's still important to vote.

5 **I know what you mean, but** isn't divorce increasing?

Speak up!

2 🔘 **1.9** Listen to each statement in Exercise 1 (a–e) and speak each response.

3 🔘 **1.9** Listen again to each statement and give a different response. Begin each reply with one of the expressions in bold.

4 🔘 **1.10** Now listen and respond to five more statements. Begin each reply with one of the expressions in bold.

Example: a

You hear: If you ask me, there are too many cars on the roads these days.

You say: I know what you mean, but everyone needs a car.

Can-do checklist

Tick what you can do.

	Can do	Need more practice
I can begin and end a conversation in a natural way.		
I can react to what I hear.		
I can maintain a conversation and ask follow-up questions.	✔	✔
I can express opinions and defend them.		

Unit2
Can I take your coat?

go to Useful language p. 79

Get ready to listen and speak

○ Which kind of restaurants do you like to go to?
- expensive restaurants ☐
- small, local restaurants ☐
- family restaurants ☐
- fast food restaurants ☐
- self-service restaurants ☐

○ What do you usually have to eat when you go out for a meal?

....

....

....

....

A Listening – In a restaurant

1 🔘11 **Listen to these questions. Tick ✓ when a waiter might ask each question.**

	Before the meal	During the meal
a	✓	
b		
c		
d		
e		
f		
g		
h		

2 🔘11 **Listen again and match each question (a–h) with a reply (1–8).**

1 Yes, I've booked a table for eight o'clock. ☐
2 No, thank you. I'll keep it with me. ☐ a
3 Oh, yes, please. It's very nice. ☐
4 Yes, it's wonderful, thank you. ☐
5 Not yet. Can we have a little more time? ☐
6 Not for me, thank you. I'm full. ☐
7 Oh, it looks lovely! Thank you. ☐
8 Yes, please. I'll have an orange juice. ☐

3 🔘12 **Look at these three short conversations. Try to guess the missing words. Then listen and check.**

1 Customer: Hello. I __booked a table__ for seven o'clock. The name's Katai.
  Waiter: Ah, yes. Follow me, please.

2 Waiter: Are you _____ ?
  Customer: Yes, for _____ I'd like the soup, please.
  Waiter: And for your _____ ?
  Customer: I'll have the salmon, thank you.
  Waiter: Very good. And would you like _____ ?
  Customer: Just some mineral water, please.

3 Waiter: Would you like _____ ?
  Customer: No, thanks. I'm full. Can I have _____ , please?

Focus on ...
describing food

Underline the positive adjectives to describe food, and circle the negative ones.

tender   bland   crispy   juicy   greasy
tough   under-done   fresh   tasty   overcooked

Think of one food that is …
salty ....
hot and spicy ....
sour ....
sweet ....
bitter ....
savoury ....

Write *S* (steak), *P* (potatoes) or *F* (fish) next to each word. Sometimes more than one answer is possible.

rare ..S..   steamed ......   sautéed ......
baked ......   medium ......   roast ......
fried ......   well-done ......   mashed ......
boiled ......   grilled ......   (stir / deep)-fried ......

B Listening – Deciding what to have

1 📀13 Imagine you are on holiday in Rome. You go to a small café for lunch. Listen to the waitress and tick ✓ the dishes she describes.

Café Filberto

Via dei Gracchi 71, Roma

Antipasti / Starter

Bruschetta   ✓   ......
Caesar salad   ....
Minestrone soup   ....

Piatti principali / Main course

Risotto Napolitano ....
Pollo Toscano   ....
Ravioli Filberto   ....
Salmone al Brodo   ....
Bistecca al Norte   ....

Dolce / Dessert

Tiramisù   ....
Chocolate tart   ....
Cheesecake   ....

Coffee or Tea   ....

€23 (service not included)

2 📀13 Write the letter of each expression (a–e) next to the correct dish in the menu. Then listen again and check.

a very light
b quite sweet
c very tasty
d a little salty
e very tender

Learning tip

You may sometimes find it hard to understand someone, especially if they have a strong accent. Remember that everyone speaks with an accent, so you need to adjust your listening. Don't stop listening – try to 'tune in' to what they are saying.

Sound smart
the schwa /ə/

The schwa is the weak vowel sound in an unstressed syllable and is pronounced /ə/. It is very common in spoken English.

1 📀14 Listen to these words. Notice the schwa.
tender   medium   under-done
wonderful   salmon   sugar

2 📀15 Now listen to these words. Underline the schwas.
waiter   reservation   potato
pasta   starter   popular

C Speaking – After a meal

Speaking strategy: Offering to pay

1 Look at these short conversations and notice the expressions in **bold**.

A: Let me **get this**, will you?
B: No, **it's on me**.

A: Shall we split the bill?
B: No. **I'll get it.** This is **my treat.**

Did you know …?

To *split the bill* means to share the cost equally. It is also called to *go Dutch*. It is quite common for people, especially young people, to *go Dutch* in many English-speaking countries.

Speak up!

2 What do you think B is saying in this conversation? Write your answers.

A: Oh, look. Here's the bill. I'll get it.
B: ....
A: Well, shall we at least split it?
B: ....
A: Are you sure?
B: ....
A: Thanks very much.
B: ....

3 🔘16 Play the recording and say your answers.

D Speaking – Dealing with problems

Speaking strategy: Complaining in a restaurant

1 🔘17 Match each complaint (a–f) with a response (1–6). Then listen and check.

a We've been waiting for our drinks for half an hour. 5
b Excuse me. These carrots are almost raw. ☐
c I'm afraid I asked for it rare, but this steak is virtually well-done. ☐
d I didn't know this dish had nuts in it. I'm allergic to them. ☐
e Don't you have any high chairs for children to sit in? ☐
f Sorry, but I asked for the bill ten minutes ago. ☐

1 Sorry, sir. I forgot to mention it. Would you like to order a different main course?
2 I'll find out what's happened to it.
3 Oh, dear. I'll get some more for you.
4 Sorry, sir. I'll bring you another one as quickly as possible.
5 Sorry, I'll bring them for you now.
6 I'm afraid not. Would a cushion do?

2 Look at the complaints (a–f) and find:

a an expression you can use to get the waiter's attention.

....

b two expressions you can use to help you complain *politely*.

....
....

Speak up!

3 🔘17 Play the recording again and take the role of the customer. Try to speak at the same time.

4 Imagine you are a customer in a restaurant. Look at these problems. Think of what you can say to the waiter. Then say your answers.

Example: a
You say: Excuse me. My soup is cold and the bread is rather hard as well.

a Your soup is cold and your bread is rather hard.
b You've been waiting for your main course for twenty minutes.
c You don't like the wine. You think it's 'corked'.
d The vegetables are under-cooked.
e You think the bill is wrong. You have been charged too much.
f You asked for sparkling mineral water, but you have still mineral water.
g You asked for green salad, but it has tomato in it. You are allergic to tomato.
h Your glass of mineral water is warm.

E Listening – Describing restaurants

1 ●18 **Martin Vickers is a TV food critic. He is talking about two restaurants he has been to recently. Listen and complete the review form.**

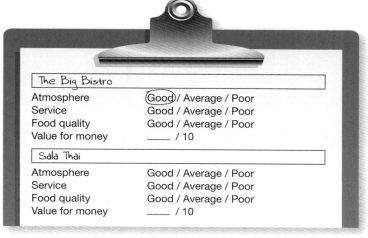

The Big Bistro

Atmosphere	(Good) / Average / Poor
Service	Good / Average / Poor
Food quality	Good / Average / Poor
Value for money	____ / 10

Sala Thai

Atmosphere	Good / Average / Poor
Service	Good / Average / Poor
Food quality	Good / Average / Poor
Value for money	____ / 10

2 ●18 **Listen again and complete Martin's notes.**

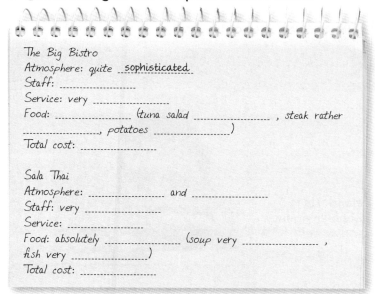

The Big Bistro
Atmosphere: quite __sophisticated__
Staff: _____
Service: very _____
Food: _____ (tuna salad _____ , steak rather
_____ , potatoes _____)
Total cost: _____

Sala Thai
Atmosphere: _____ and _____
Staff: very _____
Service: _____
Food: absolutely _____ (soup very _____ ,
fish very _____)
Total cost: _____

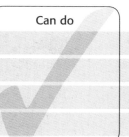

Class bonus

Make a group and role play a conversation in a restaurant.

Customers: Ask about the dishes on the menu and decide what to have. Unfortunately the meal and the service are not very good, so you will need to complain.

Waiter: Welcome your customers. Explain the dishes on the menu, take their order and serve the food.

Manager: Deal with any problems and try to keep the customers happy!

E X tra practice

Go to the *BBC Learning English* website and type 'restaurant listen' in the search box. Press enter. Then choose a link that interests you. Complete any exercises.
http://www.bbc.co.uk/worldservice/learningenglish/

Can-do checklist

Tick what you can do.

	Can do	Need more practice
I can understand explanations of dishes on a menu.		
I can offer to pay.		
I can complain effectively if there is a problem.		
I can understand restaurant reviews.		

Unit 3
I'm looking for a flat

go to Useful language p. 79

Get ready to listen and speak

- Match each type of accommodation (a–e) with a picture (1–5).
  - a a semi-detached house [5]
  - b a cottage [ ]
  - c a terraced house [ ]
  - d a detached house [ ]
  - e a block of flats [ ]

- Look at these adjectives you can use to describe houses and flats. Write P (positive) or N (negative) next to each adjective.

modern [ ]	spacious [ ]
cramped [ ]	comfortable [ ]
private [ ]	shabby [ ]
quiet [ ]	bright [ ]
noisy [ ]	messy [ ]
isolated [ ]	dingy [ ]

- Tick ✓ the adjectives that describe your home.

- How important are these factors to you when choosing a home to live in? Give each one a number (1–5). (1 = unimportant, 5 = extremely important)
  size [ ]   age [ ]   location [ ]   style [ ]   price [ ]

A Listening – Explaining your requirements

1 ●19 **Oleg has just started work in Dublin, Ireland. He is looking for a place to stay and decides to phone an agency. Listen and answer the questions.**
   a Is he going to share or live alone? _____
   b Does he want to rent or buy a property? _____

2 ●19 **Listen again and complete the form on the right.**

3 ●20 **Now listen to the second half of the conversation. Tick ✓ the property he decides to go and see.**

74 North Foley Road, Dublin
To Let: €1,250 per month
2 bedrooms, 1 bathroom
Furnished [ ]

21 Ivy Court, Dublin
To Let: €1,200 per month
2 bedrooms, 1 bathroom
Furnished [ ]

12a Joyce Street, Dublin
To Let: €1,400 per month
3 bedrooms, 2 bathrooms
Furnished [ ]

Carter Property Management Ltd.

Client requirements form

Name: [a] _Oleg Markov_ _____

Type of property: [b]flat / house

Location: [c] _____

No. bedrooms: [d] _____

No. people: [e] _____

Pets: [f]Yes / No

Smoker: [g]Yes / No

Other requirements: [h] _____

Budget: €[i] _____ (max)

B Speaking – Finding the right property

Speaking strategy: Asking about alternatives

1 Match each statement (a–e) with a response (1–5).

a Do you have anything with a larger garden? [4]
b Is there anything away from the main road? ☐
c Don't you have anything cheaper? ☐
d I'd rather have something near a better school. ☐
e I'd prefer something closer to the city centre. ☐

1 That's the most central one we have.
2 There's one in Hobart Street. That's very quiet.
3 We have one near the Rileys School. That's a good one.
4 Yes. This one has nearly half an acre.
5 I'm afraid not. That's the least expensive.

2 <u>Underline</u> the phrases in the statements (a–e) that you can use:

– to ask about alternatives.
– to express a preference.

Speak up!

3 Imagine a property agent is showing you various properties for rent. What can you say in the situations below? Say your answers.

Example: a
You say: It's nice, but it's a bit small. Do you have anything a little larger?

a Small – larger?
b Noisy neighbourhood
c No garden
d No garage
e Too expensive

Focus on …
comparatives and superlatives

Complete the sentences using the comparative or superlative form of the words in brackets.

a I'd like something with a _____bigger_____ (big) garden, if possible.
b The one on Park Avenue is _____ (expensive) of the three.
c I think this one is _____ (good) than the others.
d Don't you have anything _____ (near) the sea?
e This one is the _____ (nice) one we've seen.
f Do you have something which is _____ (convenient) for the shops?

C Listening – Checking the financial side

1 ⊙ ⏯21 Look at these questions. Then listen to this property agent in the US. Which questions does he answer?

	Finances	
a	How much is the rent?	✔
b	When is the rent due?	☐
c	How much deposit is required?	☐
d	Will I get all my deposit back?	☐
e	Are bills included?	☐

2 ⊙ ⏯21 Listen again and answer each question.

D Listening – Making sure of the facts

1 **22 Read these questions. Then listen to the property agent's replies. Write the letter of each reply (a–f) next to the correct question.**

Tenancy agreement
1 How long is the rental agreement?   ------
2 Will the rent go up?   ------
3 Is insurance included?   ------
4 Can I sub-let?   ------
5 How much notice must I give if I want
   to leave early?   ..a.
6 Who do I contact if there is a problem?   ------

2 **22 Look at the statements below. Tick ✓ True or False for each statement. Then listen again and check your answers.**

	True	False
a You need to give two months' notice.		✓
b Contents insurance is not included.		
c The rent may go up after the lease expires.		
d You should pay for repairs yourself.		
e The rental agreement starts from the day you move in.		
f You will be evicted if you break the terms of your tenancy agreement.		

E Speaking – Getting what you want

Speaking strategy: Making requests and asking for permission

1 **Look at the expressions in bold below. Which expressions can you use:**

a to ask permission to do something?
b to ask someone to do something?

Is it OK if I have broadband installed?
Could you send someone to repair the cooker, please?
Would you mind if I got cable TV?
Would you mind fix**ing** the tap in the bathroom?
I was wondering if I could paint the kitchen a different colour.

Speak up!

2 **Imagine you have just moved in to a rented flat and want to make some changes. Think of what you can say when you call your landlord to ask permission. Then say your answers.**

Example: a
You say: Would you mind if I painted the lounge white? It's green at the moment and I'd like something a little brighter.

a Lounge green – white
b Satellite TV
c Change phone company
d New sofa
e Broadband Internet

3 **Now imagine that you have discovered lots of problems. Think of what you can say to ask the landlord to fix them. Then say your answers.**

Example: a
You say: Could you send someone to repair the washing machine, please? It's stopped working.

a The washing machine has stopped working.
b Your bedroom window is broken.
c The heating doesn't work properly.
d The garden is a mess.
e The front doorbell doesn't work.

F Listening – Dealing with problems

🔘 123 Lucy and Samir are tenants in the same block of flats in London. They each have a problem and call the rental agent, Mr Lee. Listen and complete the chart.

		Lucy	Samir
1	What's the problem?	a The cooker is broken.	d _____
2	When did it start?	b _____	e _____
3	What does Mr Lee promise?	c _____	f _____

G Speaking – Overcoming difficulties

Speaking strategy: Making your point more forcefully

1 🔘 123 Listen again to Lucy and Samir complain to Mr Lee. Tick ✓ the expressions you hear.

I really must insist that you do something about this immediately. ☐
I'm not very happy about this at all. ☐
I'd like to know what you are going to do about it. ☐

Speak up!

2 **Imagine you are a tenant with the following problems. Complain to your rental agent and make your point forcefully. Use the expressions above and say your answers.**

Example: a
You say: I told you four days ago that the roof in my bedroom leaks, but nobody has been to repair it yet. I'm not very happy about this at all. When are you going to send someone to fix it?

a Roof in bedroom leaks (told four days ago)
b Smoke alarm broken (told two weeks ago)
c Gardening not done (for two months)
d Kitchen sink blocked (since last week)
e Saw mouse in kitchen (last night)

Class bonus

Work with a partner. One person is a tenant and the other is a rental agent.
Tenant: You moved in to your apartment last month. There are some things you would like to change and there are also some problems you want your rental agent to fix. You call your rental agent.
Rental agent: Listen to your tenant and respond to each request or complaint.

E X tra practice

Go to www.google.com and type *renting accommodation listen* in the search box. Choose a link and watch or listen to any information you find.

Can-do checklist

Tick what you can do.

	Can do	Need more practice
I can explain my accommodation requirements.		
I can ask about alternatives to help me find the right place.		
I can ask detailed questions about costs and legal requirements.		
I can deal with problems and complain effectively.		

Unit 4
I'd like a refund, please

go to Useful language p. 79

Get ready to listen and speak

Match each word (a–h) with a definition (1–8).

a a credit voucher [2]   e an extended warranty [ ]
b a refund [ ]   f faulty [ ]
c to exchange [ ]   g to haggle [ ]
d a receipt [ ]   h a bargain [ ]

1 **(n)** a piece of paper you receive that proves what you bought, when, and how much you paid

2 **(n)** a piece of paper from a shop that allows you to buy goods up to the value shown

3 **(n)** something on sale at a much lower price than normal

4 **(v)** to change something you bought for something else of similar value

5 **(v)** to negotiate the price of something before buying it

6 **(n)** money you receive when you return something

7 **(n)** a guarantee that lasts longer than the normal period

8 **(adj)** describing an item which is not working correctly

24 Listen to eight statements. For each statement, tick ✓ who you think is speaking.

	Customer	Shop assistant
a	[ ]	[ ]
b	[ ]	[ ]
c	[ ]	[ ]
d	[ ]	[ ]
e	[ ]	[ ]
f	[ ]	[ ]
g	[ ]	[ ]
h	[ ]	[ ]

A Listening – In a shop

Customer Service

1 25 Listen to Maribel, a Brazilian au pair working in London, return an item to a shop. Answer the questions.

a What item is Maribel returning? _A blouse_
b What is the problem with it? _____
c What does Maribel ask for? _____
d Why doesn't the assistant agree? _____
e What does Maribel decide to do? _____

2 25 Listen again and (circle) five mistakes in this complaint form. The first one has been done for you.

Haywards Department Store

Complaint Form CS284

Item:	Ray Nichols (jeans)
Purchased:	Last month
Receipt:	Yes [ ] No [✓]
Problem:	Item has shrunk (only washed twice).
Action taken:	Credit voucher given.

B Speaking – Returning items

Speaking strategy: Making a complaint in a shop

1 Look at this extract from Maribel's conversation in the shop.

Assistant: We can't accept responsibility.
Maribel: Well, I'm sorry, but that's not good enough.

2 Notice the expressions in bold you can use when you want to complain.

I'm sorry, but this camera doesn't work properly.
I'm afraid that this phone doesn't work properly.
Sorry, but this phone is broken and I've only had it two weeks.

Speak up!

3 Imagine you are a customer in a shop. Use the information below to complain to the shop assistant.

Example: a
You say: Hello. I bought this notebook computer yesterday, but I'm afraid that the display doesn't work.

a You bought a notebook computer yesterday, but the display doesn't work.
b The radio you bought last week has stopped working.
c A friend gave you a vase for your birthday, but it is cracked.
d The shoes you bought two months ago are already falling apart.
e Your new tennis racquet broke the first time you used it.

Learning tip

Take care with the way you use your voice. For example, if you need to complain, try to sound friendly rather than aggressive. Don't raise your voice or appear out of control.

Did you know ...?

A recent survey of 30,000 customers in 30 countries revealed big differences in how likely customers are to complain.

Most likely to complain	Least likely to complain
Sweden 41%	Taiwan 1%
UK 36%	Saudi Arabia 3%
Australia 30%	China 4%
Canada 26%	Poland 5%
US 23%	Russia 6%

Sound smart
Showing emotion

1 🔊 **26** The *way* you say something can be as important as *what* you actually say. Listen to this sentence spoken in two different ways.

A: I saw John today.
B: I saw John today.

Notice how A's voice goes up and down more, showing excitement and interest. B's voice stays very flat, making him sound bored and uninterested.

2 🔊 **27** Listen to six people each say *Good morning. How are you?* Match each speaker (1–6) with how you think they feel.

1   friendly
2   worried
3   angry
4   bored
5   interested
6   tired

3 🔊 **27** Listen again and repeat each sentence, copying the same intonation.

C Listening – Understanding shop policy

🔊 **28** Barbara is the manager of an electrical shop. Listen to her explain the shop's policy on refunds and exchanges. Tick ✓ True or False for each statement.

		True	False
a	Damaged and faulty items must be returned straight away.	☐	✓
b	You can either have a refund or exchange the item.	☐	☐
c	You must have a receipt.	☐	☐
d	You have to pay a small administration charge for items that need to be repaired.	☐	☐
e	Unwanted items can be refunded or exchanged if returned in under two weeks.	☐	☐
f	If you return an unwanted item after two weeks of purchase, then no refund is possible.	☐	☐

D Listening – Finding out more about a product

1 🔊 **29** Listen to six questions this customer asks. Count the number of words in each question. A contraction (like *Where's*) is two words.

a ⬚5⬚ b ☐ c ☐ d ☐ e ☐ f ☐

2 🔊 **29** Listen again and write each question.

a What size is the screen? ☐
b .... ☐
c .... ☐
d .... ☐
e .... ☐
f .... ☐

3 🔊 **29** Listen again and repeat each question using the same stress and rhythm. What product do you think the customer is asking about?

....

4 🔊 **30** Now listen to the sales assistant's answers. Write the number of each answer (1–6) next to the correct question (a–f) in Exercise 2.

5 🔊 **31** The customer sees two new mobile phones on sale. Listen to the sales assistant talk about them and complete the missing information.

S340

4G
Fast ᵃ ....Internet....
Download ᵇ .... clips
ᶜ .... mega pixel camera
ᵈ .... video calling

410i

MP3 player + ᵉ ....
Stereo sound
Can store ᶠ .... + songs
Full ᵍ .... – like a pocket PC
ʰ .... gigabyte hard drive

Learning tip

If you want to check you have understood something correctly, repeat the important details to the speaker. Make sure your voice goes up at the end of the sentence to make it clear you are asking for confirmation.

E Listening – Bargaining

1 🔊32 **Pierre is at a market in London, haggling with a stallholder. Listen and tick ✓ which sentences you hear the stallholder say.**

a That's £35 to you. ✓
  It's £35 to you. ☐
b Let's say 30 pound, then. How's that? ☐
  Let's say 30 pound, then. What about that? ☐
c It's a bargain, I promise. ☐
  It's a bargain, I promise you. ☐
d That is a cash price! ☐
  That is the best price! ☐
e It's a deal. ☐
  It's not dear. ☐

2 🔊32 **Listen again and complete Pierre's sentences.**

a It's a bit more than I wanted to _____pay_____ .
b Is that your _____ ?
c Can't you _____ any better?
d How much _____ ?
e Well, _____ you £20 for it.

F Speaking – Negotiating the price

Speaking strategy: Reaching an agreement

1 **Look at these expressions you can use to accept or reject a price.**

To accept a price:	To reject a price:
That's OK with me.	No, I can't pay that.
OK. That's fine.	Sorry, it's too much.
It's a deal.	It's not worth that.

Speak up!

2 🔊33 **Imagine you are at a market. Listen and accept or reject each offer on price.**

Example: a
You hear: You can have the desk for $45.
You say: Sorry, it's too much. Can't you do any better?

Can-do checklist

Tick what you can do.

	Can do	Need more practice
I can make a complaint in a shop.		
I can understand a shop's returns policy.		
I can ask questions about various products.		
I can bargain and reach an agreement.		

Unit 5
Is there anything on?

Get ready to listen and speak

○ Do you watch a lot of TV?
  Not really. I only watch programmes I like. ☐
  I watch quite a lot of TV. ☐
  Yes, I'm a real telly addict. ☐

○ Unscramble the letters to find ten types of film.
  Can you think of an example for each one?
  a   ecdoym   _comedy_
  b   orhror   _____
  c   eiccnse tiiocfn _____
  d   rwa   _____
  e   itlhlerr   _____
  f   tfasayn   _____
  g   iaocnt   _____
  h   ovle osryt   _____
  i   tweerns   _____
  j   aatinoimn   _____

Did you know …?

Although most internationally famous movies are made in English, every year an Oscar is given for the Best Foreign Language Film. Past winners include _Crouching Tiger, Hidden Dragon_ (Taiwan), _Life is Beautiful_ (Italy), _Babette's Feast_ (Denmark) and _Tsotsi_ (South Africa).

○ Do you prefer to watch films at the cinema or at home on DVD?

go to Useful language p. 80

A Listening – A film review

1 ◉ 34 **Listen to Matthew Jenkins, a film critic, talk about a new film. Note down who these people are.**

Jane Martins   _A maid in a large country house_
Charles Danton _____
Helen Richards _____
Peter Kite   _____
Kevin Hadley   _____

2 ◉ 34 **Look at the statements below. Tick ✓ True, False or Don't know for each statement. Then listen again and check.**

		True	False	Don't know
a	The film takes place in the north of England.	☐	☐	✓
b	It is based on a true story.	☐	☐	☐
c	Both the main actors are very good.	☐	☐	☐
d	The ending is rather weak.	☐	☐	☐
e	It is Kevin Hadley's first film.	☐	☐	☐
f	The movie is only suitable for adults.	☐	☐	☐

B Speaking – Describing films

Speaking strategy: Talking about films

1 Write *P* (positive) or *N* (negative) next to each word or expression.

heart-warming ......P...... ☐
well acted ...... ☐
lots of twists and turns ...... ☐
too long ...... ☐
a bit boring ...... ☐
very surprising ...... ☐
gripping ...... ☐
utterly believable ...... ☐
original ...... ☐
predictable ...... ☐

2 🔊 **34** Listen to the film review again. Tick ✓ the words and expressions in Exercise 1 that you hear.

Speak up!

3 Think of a film you like. Look at the questions below and make notes.

My favourite film

What is the plot?

Who are the main characters?

How does it end?

Who was it directed by?

Can you remember any of the actors?

Is it well acted?

Were there any special effects?

Do you like the soundtrack?

Why do you like this film?

4 Now talk about the film. If possible, record yourself and play back the recording afterwards. Can you identify any areas to improve?

C Listening – Describing TV programmes

1 🔊 **35** Listen to six people each describe a TV programme they enjoy. Write the number of each speaker (1–6) next to the type of programme they are describing.

...... news ...... crime series ...... soap opera ...... drama
...... talk show ...... quiz show ...1... cartoon ...... documentary
...... nature ...... cookery ...... sport ...... comedy

2 🔊 **35** Look at the audioscript on page 90 and listen again. Underline any words and phrases that help you identify the type of programme.

3 🔊 **36** Listen to five people give their opinion on different TV programmes. Write *P* (positive) or *N* (negative).

a ..P..　b ......　c ......　d ......　e ......

4 🔊 **36** Listen again and note the key words that helped you identify each comment as positive or negative.

a I'm really into it. ....
b ....
c ....
d ....
e ....

Learning tip

Listening for opinions is a useful skill. Try to notice if the speaker is using positive or negative words, and ask yourself how these reflect their viewpoint. If you hear mostly negative words, then the speaker's opinion is likely to be unfavourable. Similarly, a lot of positive words would indicate approval.

D Listening – Listening to the news

1 🔘 37 **Listen to the radio news headlines. How many different stories are mentioned?**

----

2 🔘 37 **Tick ✓ the topics that are mentioned. Then listen again and check.**

entertainment ☐   science ☐
sport ☐   the environment ☐
politics ☐   space ☐
the economy ✓   education ☐
culture ☐

Learning tip

If possible, look for any visual clues that could help you. For example, the pictures that accompany the news on television can help you understand the topic of each news item.

3 🔘 37 **Listen again and write down the key points in each headline.**

<u>Downturn for EU + North American economies. China</u>
<u>dominant superpower by 2025.</u>

----

4 🔘 38 **Now listen to the main story in more detail. Answer the questions.**

a   What organization carried out the research?
   <u>The Global Studies Institute</u>
b   Has China overtaken the world's major economies yet?
   ----
c   By when is China expected to be the dominant economic power? _____
d   When did China's economic reforms begin?
   ----
e   How much of the American market is China predicted to have? _____
f   How much of the European market is China predicted to have? _____
g   Who is Tim Robbins? _____

E Speaking – Talking about the news

Speaking strategy: Summarizing

1 Which of these summaries of the news story about China is most accurate? _____

a   China's economy is going to grow stronger over the next thirty years, but it will not overtake the economies of America and Europe.
b   China has the fastest growing economy in the world today. It has already replaced America and Europe as the biggest industrial and commercial centre in the world.
c   China's economy has been growing quickly for the last thirty years. According to one report, it will not be long before it becomes the biggest economy in the world.

Speak up!

2 🔘 39 **Listen to this news story and write down the main points. Then give a brief summary of the story, using your notes as a guide.**

<u>It's about</u>

<u>A report by</u>   <u>found that</u>

F Listening – Making predictions

1 You are going to listen to two news reports about global warming. Tick ✓ the words you think you may hear.

food ☐   temperatures ☐
century ☐   traffic ☐
scientists ☐   education ☐
prices ☐   shopping ☐
falling ☐   friendship ☐
loss ☐   rise ☐
holiday ☐   sea ice ☐
recover ☐

2 🔘40 Listen to the first report. Circle the words above that are mentioned.

3 🔘41 Now listen to the second report. Each time there is a pause, note what you think will come next.

Sound smart
Stress and rhythm

1 🔘40 Look at the first report on global warming. Listen again and notice how the underlined words have more stress.

A group of top European and Australian scientists say that temperatures will rise much faster than previously predicted, possibly by as much as six per cent by the end of the century. They also say that the record loss of sea ice over recent years means that the earth may no longer be able to recover.

2 🔘41 Find the audioscript on page 91 for the second report on global warming. Listen and underline the words and expressions that should have more stress.

3 Read both reports aloud. Stress the important words.

E X tra practice

Go to the *BBC Learning English* website and click on 'News'. Choose some news stories to watch or listen to. You could also go to the *Voice of America Special English* website to watch or listen to more news stories.
http://www.bbc.co.uk/worldservice/learningenglish/
http://www.voanews.com/specialenglish/

Class bonus

1 Make a group and plan a radio show. You need one presenter, one reporter and one reviewer. Decide what stories to cover and each prepare your roles.

Presenter: It is your job to read the main headlines and present the show.

Reporter: You need to report in detail on the main story of the day.

Reviewer: You need to give a review of a film and a TV programme.

2 When you are ready, present your show to the class.

Can-do checklist

Tick what you can do.

	Can do	Need more practice
I can describe and discuss films and TV programmes.		
I can summarize main news stories.		
I can make predictions about what I will hear.		

Unit 6
I've got a pain in my arm

Get ready to listen and speak

- Make a list of as many common health problems as you can.
  a headache, a sore throat,
  _____

- Match each word (a–f) with a picture (1–6).
  a an injection 5   b an inhaler ☐   c crutches ☐
  d antibiotics ☐   e a cast ☐   f a thermometer ☐

- Tick ✓ the health problems below that you or someone you know suffers from.
  skin problems ☐
  insomnia ☐
  asthma ☐
  hay fever ☐
  migraines ☐
  high blood pressure ☐
  stress ☐

go to Useful language p. 80

A Listening – At the doctor's

1 ●42 Complete these questions a doctor might ask a patient. Then listen to the conversation and check.

1 What seems to be the ____trouble____ ?
2 Do you _____ when it started?
3 Where does it _____ exactly?
4 Is it _____ if I do this?
5 Are you _____ to anything?
6 Have you got any other _____ ?
7 Have you been _____ anything for it?

2 ●42 Write the answers to these questions. Then listen to the conversation again and check your answers.

a What problem does Mohammed have?
   He has a terrible pain in his shoulder.
b When did it start?
   _____
c What other symptoms does he have?
   _____
d Has he been taking any medicine for it?
   _____
e What action does the doctor want to take?
   _____

Did you know ...?

A *dermatologist* specializes in skin problems.
An *ophthalmologist* treats eye diseases.
A *paediatrician* is a specialist in children's health.
A *psychiatrist* specializes in mental health.
A *cardiologist* is a heart specialist.

Focus on ...
describing health problems

Write each word in the correct category.

| dry | stabbing | dull | tickly | shooting | chesty |

Words to describe a cough:
dry

Words to describe a pain:

Complete the sentences, using the words below.

| sprained | runny | blotches | bleed | sore | feverish |
| temperature | numb | swollen | itchy | rash | |

a My foot is badly ___ swollen ___ .
b I need some tissues. I've got a _____ nose.
c Have you got anything for a _____ throat?
d Mike often has a nose _____ in the morning.
e Aunt Sophia has _____ her ankle.
f I've got a high _____ .
g I feel very _____ . I'm sweating a lot.
h I have no feeling in my fingers. They're _____ .
i I've got a bad _____ on my arm.
j What are these _____ all over my neck?
k My legs are very _____ . I can't stop scratching.

B Speaking – Explaining what's wrong

Speaking strategy: Describing symptoms

1 **Look at this extract from Mohammed's conversation with the doctor. Notice how he describes the problem.**

Doctor: Now, what seems to be the trouble?
Mohammed: **I've got a** terrible **pain in my** shoulder.

Here are some other phrases you can use to describe your symptoms.

I think I'm **suffering from** stress.
I'm **coming down with** the flu.
My arm **aches**.

Speak up!

2 🔊 443 **Imagine you are at the doctor's. Listen to each question and use the ideas below to have two conversations.**

You hear: What seems to be the trouble?
           a
You say: I think I'm coming down with the flu.

Conversation 1
a the flu, b yesterday, c since yesterday morning, d runny nose, sore throat, headache, e a little, f some aspirin

Conversation 2
a pain / back, b at the bottom, c last Sunday, d No, e Yes, very, f some pain killers

3 🔊 444 **Now listen and use your own ideas to answer each question.**

4 **Imagine you have the following health problems. Make a list of symptoms and then explain what's wrong to the doctor.**

a the flu
b stress
c food poisoning

a bad cough
b _____
c _____

Learning tip

In this type of situation, don't worry too much about making mistakes. It doesn't matter if your English isn't perfect. It's better to keep speaking and get your message across.

C Listening – Getting a diagnosis

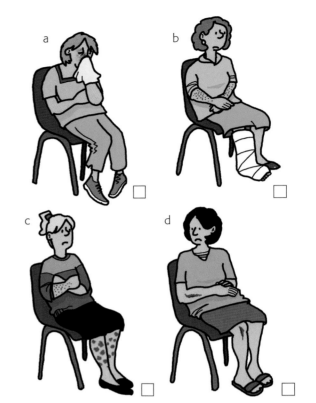

1 🔘 45 **Listen to Sharon Maurice talk to her doctor about a health problem. Tick ✓ the picture on the right that shows Sharon.**

2 a What exactly is wrong with Sharon?

   ----

   b What does the doctor think is the cause?

   ----

3 🔘 45 **Look at the statements below. Tick ✓ True or False for each statement. Then listen again and check your answers.**

		True	False
a	The blotches are all over Sharon's body.	☐	✓
b	They are getting worse.	☐	☐
c	She noticed them two weeks ago.	☐	☐
d	She also has a rash, which is very itchy.	☐	☐
e	It's caused by an allergic reaction to her cat.	☐	☐
f	The doctor prescribes some tablets.	☐	☐
g	He expects both problems to clear up quickly.	☐	☐
h	Sharon has to go back in two weeks.	☐	☐

D Listening – Understanding the doctor's instructions

1 🔘 46 **Dr Vasquez is a doctor in Texas, US. He is speaking to a patient. Listen and answer the questions.**

   a What's wrong with the patient?

   ----

   b Why doesn't Dr Vasquez prescribe antibiotics?

   ----

   c What advice does he give?

   ----

2 🔘 47 **Listen to Dr Vasquez diagnose three more patients. Complete the chart.**

	Diagnosis	Instructions
Patient 1	a chest _____	two tablets _____ a day for _____ days
Patient 2	a mild case of _____	use an _____ / come back _____
Patient 3	a very bad _____	take _____ spoonfuls every _____ hours / don't _____ / come back in _____

3 🔘 48 **Imagine you are a patient of Dr Vasquez. Listen and tick ✓ the correct statements. Put a cross ✗ next to the incorrect statements.**

   a You should take two tablets, twice a day, before meals. ✗   The problem should go in a couple of days. ☐
   b You shouldn't drink alcohol, but coffee is OK. ☐   You should start eating small portions of food. ☐
   c You need to exercise more often. ☐   You shouldn't drink alcohol or milk. ☐

E Speaking – Reacting to news

Speaking strategy: Showing concern and relief

1 <u>Underline</u> the expressions to express concern and relief.

Dr Vasquez: You have some sort of virus, I'm afraid.
Patient: Oh, dear. Really? Are you sure?
Dr Vasquez: Yes. I don't think it's too serious, though.
Patient: Thank goodness for that!

2 Write *C* (concern) or *R* (relief) next to each expression.

Thank goodness for that! __R__   How awful! ......
Oh, no. That's terrible. ......   Phew! ......
Oh, I'm sorry to hear that. ......   What a relief! ......
Well, that's good news. ......
Oh, dear. Really? ......

Speak up!

3 49 Listen to eight statements and respond, expressing concern or relief.

Example: a
You hear: My blood pressure is very high.
You say: Oh, I'm sorry to hear that.

Sound smart
Linking – /w/ and /j/

1 50 Listen to these sentences. Notice that a /w/ or /j/ sound is added when a word ending in a vowel sound is followed by a word beginning with a vowel sound.

I'll give you /w/ a prescription.
The /j/ operation was a success.

2 Say these sentences aloud. Which words do you think are linked with /w/ or /j/ ? Some sentences have more than one example.

　　　　/w/　　/w/
a Are you allergic to anything?
b Come back at the end of the week and we'll see if you're better.
c It's not serious, so I don't want to give you any tablets.
d The exercise will help you a lot, so please do it!
e Who is your regular doctor?
f You are quite ill, I'm afraid.
g The good news is that we aren't going to operate.
h Your knee is a lot better now.

3 51 Listen and check. Then listen again and repeat each sentence. Practise linking the sounds.

E X tra practice

Imagine you are ill. Make a list of your symptoms and tell your doctor. If possible, record what you say and listen to yourself afterwards. Identify areas to improve, e.g. your grammar or pronunciation.

Class bonus

Half the class are doctors; the other half are patients.
Patients: Imagine you are ill. Make a list of your symptoms. Then find a doctor and describe what's wrong. Listen carefully to the doctor's diagnosis and instructions.
Doctors: Listen to your patients describe their health problems. Ask questions to help you make an accurate diagnosis. Then prescribe some medicine and give instructions.

Can-do checklist

Tick what you can do.

	Can do	Need more practice
I can describe a range of symptoms accurately.	✔	✔
I can participate actively in a consultation, answering questions.		
I can understand the doctor's diagnosis and instructions.		
I can react to news, showing concern and relief.		

Unit 7
I could do with a break

Get ready to listen and speak

- Who do you prefer to travel with?
  with family ☐ with friends ☐ alone ☐ with your partner ☐

- Which is the best way to travel?
  with a tour, where everything is organized for you ☐
  just booking hotels and transport in advance ☐
  with no fixed plan, making all the arrangements yourself en route ☐

- Match each type of holiday (a–f) with a picture (1–6).
  a a cruise [6]   b a skiing holiday ☐   c a holiday by the seaside ☐
  d a city break ☐   e a camping holiday ☐   f an activity holiday ☐

go to Useful language p. 80

A Listening – Types of holiday

1 ▶ 52 **Listen and write the type of holiday each speaker prefers.**

1 a holiday by the seaside _____
2 _____
3 _____
4 _____
5 _____
6 _____

Learning tip

Listening for key words and phrases is an important skill. Try to group the words and phrases you hear into similar topics or themes. For example, if you hear *class*, *exam*, *teacher* and *homework*, then the topic might be *school*.

2 ▶ 52 **Listen again and complete the key words and expressions that help identify each type of holiday each speaker is describing.**

1: relaxing on the ____beach____ , __swimming__ , playing in the ____sea____ , making __sand castles__

2: looking around _____ , going to _____ , hopping on a _____ bus

3: catching the _____ , top of the _____ , _____ down, fantastic _____

4: _____ riding, _____ , _____-riding, doing _____ things

5: being _____ , waking up in a _____ , going _____

6: sit on the _____ and relax, look _____

B Listening – Choosing a holiday

1 ●53 Simon and Jenny Carter are booking their summer holiday with a travel agent. Listen and find six mistakes in the booking information form. The first one has been done for you.

TrailBlazers

Customer Booking Information

Booking Ref:	9873459

Client:	Mr & Mrs Carter

Flights

From London (LHR) to Vancouver (YVR)

June ~~13th~~ 12th	AC855	Dep 12:30	Arr 14:25	No. people: 2	Cost per person: £780

From Calgary (YYC) to London (LHR)

June 20th	AC852	Dep 22:00	Arr 01:55		

Hotels		Cost (prpn / breakfast included)
Metropolitan Vancouver 4*	No. of nights: 2	£160
Emerald Lake Lodge 4*	No. of nights: 2	£150
Fairmont Jasper Park Lodge 4*	No. of nights: 2	£250
Westin Calgary 4*	No. of nights: 1	£94

Car hire:	(Compact) £25 per day

This quote valid for 14 days.

2 ●53 **Listen again and answer these questions.**

a What does *prpn* mean? _____
b How long does it take to drive from:
  Vancouver to Lake Louise? _____
  Lake Louise to Jasper? _____
  Jasper to Calgary? _____
c What can you do in these places?
  Jasper National Park: _____
  _____
  Calgary: _____
  _____

Class bonus

Half the class are travel agents; the other half are tourists.

Tourists: Find a travel agent and find out what holidays they have to offer. Ask for detailed information before you book.

Travel agents: Think of three different holidays you want to offer and note as many details as you can. Then try to sell your holiday to as many tourists as possible.

C Speaking – Travel tips

Speaking strategy: Making recommendations

1 Look at the expressions below. Which can you use:

   a to recommend someone does something?
   b to recommend someone *doesn't* do something?

   1 It's well worth …ing $\boxed{a}$
   2 Don't bother …ing ☐
   3 You should definitely … ☐
   4 It's not really worth …ing ☐
   5 I recommend (that) you … ☐
   6 I wouldn't … if I were you. ☐
   7 I recommend …ing. ☐

2 ● 53 Listen again to the conversation at the travel agent's. Tick ✓ the expressions you hear.

Speak up!

3 ● 54 Imagine you are in your hometown and a tourist asks you some questions. Listen and reply, using your own ideas.

Example: a
You hear: Can you recommend a good place to stay?
You say: Yes, there's a good hotel on Clarence Road. It's right in the centre. I don't think it's very expensive. You could try that.

Focus on …   ab C def
phrasal verbs

Complete the sentences using these particles.

around	to	~~off~~	back	in	out of	back	up	off

a What time shall we set ……off…… tomorrow?
b We'll pick you ……………… at six.
c I forgot to bring ……………… any souvenirs, I'm afraid.
d I'm looking forward ……………… this trip.
e You can't check ……………… before 2 pm.
f The best way to get ……………… the city is by tram.
g We checked ……………… the hotel and left.
h All my friends saw me ……………… at the airport.
i I didn't get ……………… to the hotel until very late.

D Speaking – Booking a day trip

Speaking strategy: Asking for detailed information

1 You can ask these questions if you want to go on a day trip or excursion.

What time does it leave?
Where does it leave from?
How long does it last?
What exactly is included?
Are there any hidden extras?

Speak up!

2 ● 55 Imagine you are on holiday and a tour guide is trying to sell you an excursion. Listen and respond to each sentence you hear, using the prompts below.

You hear: Do you want to go on a night cruise?
a
You say: That might be nice. How long does it last?

   a How long?
   b Where / leave from?
   c What time / leave?
   d What / included?
   e Hidden extras?
   f OK / think about it.

3 Look at this advert for another cruise. What questions can you ask for more information?

What time does it leave? ………………………………
…………………………………………………………………
…………………………………………………………………

Pharos Island
cruise €35
Half-day relaxing cruise
Departs from Paphos harbour
Route: west to Coral Bay
On-board barbecue with drinks

(Parascending € 15 extra)

E Listening – Renting a car

1 🔊 **56** **Listen and complete these questions you can ask when you want to rent a car.**

a What _____range_____ of cars do you have? ☐
b Is _____ included? ☐
c Do I have to pay an _____ if I have an accident? ☐
d Can I hire a car _____ ? ☐
e Is there a _____ limit? ☐
f Do you provide _____ ? ☐
g Is _____ cover included? ☐
h What _____ do I need? ☐

2 🔊 **57** **Listen and write the number of each response (1–8) next to the correct question (a–h).**

3 🔊 **58** **Listen to Laura in Italy rent a car at Dublin airport. Complete the information.**

VW Polo		
Class: Economy / €ᵃ_____89_____ pw		
Ford Fiesta		
Class: ᵇ_____ / €ᶜ_____ pw		
Toyota Corolla		
Class: ᵈ_____ / €ᵉ_____ pw		
Toyota Avensis		
Class: Full-sized / €ᶠ_____ pw		

4 🔊 **58** **Read these questions. Try to remember the answers. Then listen again and check.**

a How long does she want to rent a car? _For a week._
b Why doesn't she want the VW Polo? _____
c Why doesn't she rent the Ford Fiesta? _____
d How much does she finally pay? _____
e Why is this cheaper than the advertised price? _____

Did you know …?

In British English, you *rent* or *hire* cars, bikes, DVDs and electronic equipment. In American English, *hire* is only used for people.

Sound smart
Missing sounds – /t/, /d/ and /h/

1 🔊 **59** Listen to these questions. Notice that the sounds /t/, /d/ and /h/ often disappear in connected speech.
Why doesn('t) she ren(t) the For(d) Fiesta?
Did (h)e say (h)e'd (h)ave the car for nex(t) week?

2 Look at sentences a–h. Which /t/, /d/ and /h/ sounds do you think are not pronounced?
a I've go(t) jus(t) one question.
b You didn't say you couldn't swim.
c We could go tomorrow.
d You must be tired.
e Have you played before?
f I managed to talk to her last night.
g Are you taking him to the station?
h I didn't know the answer, so I kept quiet.

3 🔊 **60** Listen and check. Then listen again and repeat.

E 🅧 tra practice

Go to http://www.bbc.co.uk/worldservice/learningenglish/ and type *rent car video* in the search box. Watch the video and complete the exercises.

Can-do checklist

Tick what you can do.

	Can do	Need more practice
I can understand detailed information about travel arrangements.	✔	✔
I can make and respond to recommendations.		
I can ask for detailed travel information.		
I can enquire about renting a car.		

Unit 8
It's an amazing place!

- Where was the last place you visited on a sightseeing trip? Did you enjoy it?

- What is the best way to look around a city? Number these options in order (1–4).

  on your own ....

  with a friend ....

  with a group of friends ....

  on a guided tour ....

- Put each verb in the correct place.

go on   work out   travel   ~~do~~   have

  a ___do___ some sightseeing / everything on your list

  b .... a look around / a rest

  c .... where you are / what to do

  d .... a guided tour / an excursion

  e .... around by bus / independently

go to Useful language p. 81

A Listening – A short break

1 🔊 **61** **Mark is asking his friend Emmanuel for advice on going to Paris. Listen and tick ✓ the topics Emmanuel mentions.**

accommodation ✓   food ☐   money ☐   safety ☐
transport ☐   nightlife ☐   weather ☐   attractions ☐

2 🔊 **61** **Tick ✓ True or False for each statement. Then listen again and check.**

	True	False
a Mark is going to Paris next weekend.	☐	✓
b He hasn't found anywhere to stay yet.	☐	☐
c Taking the Metro is easy but expensive.	☐	☐
d It's possible to walk to most of the main sights.	☐	☐
e Changing money can be difficult.	☐	☐
f Emmanuel thinks Paris is more dangerous than London.	☐	☐

3 a Where does Emmanuel say Mark can find a cheap place to stay?

----

b Why is it a lively area of the city?

Did you know …?

The worldwide tourist industry is worth over 500 billion euros a year. The most popular tourist destination in the world is Paris. Over 25 million people a year visit the city. However, the fastest-growing region for tourism is Asia.

Focus on … abcdef
describing places

Match the adjectives which have a similar meaning.

a crowded   vibrant
b fascinating   popular
c lively   international
d touristy   beautiful
e picturesque   dirty
f pricey   packed
g cosmopolitan   historic
h peaceful   interesting
i trendy   expensive
j old-fashioned   quiet
k polluted   fashionable

B Speaking – Finding out information (1)

Speaking strategy: Making polite requests

1 Look at this extract. <u>Underline</u> the phrase Mark uses to ask Emmanuel for information about Paris.

As you're from Paris, I was wondering if you could give me some tips?

2 Here are some more expressions you can use. Notice the expressions in **bold**.

Do you think you could suggest a few places to see?
I don't suppose you know anywhere good to stay?
I wonder if you'd mind giving me a bit of advice?

Speak up!

3 Imagine you are going on a short sightseeing trip. You know someone who comes from the place you are visiting. Ask politely for information.

Example: a
You say: I was wondering if you could suggest a good place to stay?

a accommodation
b weather
c transport
d safety
e money
f food
g nightlife
h shopping

C Speaking – Finding out information (2)

Speaking strategy: Asking for recommendations

1 <u>Underline</u> the expressions you can use to ask for recommendations.

<u>Do you think I should</u> exchange money at a bank or bureau de change?
Is it worth visiting the aquarium?
Do you think it's a good idea to walk to the castle, or is it too far?
Would you recommend going to the National Museum?

Speak up!

2 Imagine you are on holiday in Singapore. There are lots of things to do and you don't have much time. Look at the pictures and ask the hotel receptionist for some recommendations.

Example: a
You say: Is it worth going on a sightseeing bus?

D Listening – Following a talk

1 Before you listen, make a list of everything you know about Peru.

Learning tip

By asking yourself what you know about a topic before you listen, you are better prepared. Whenever possible, try to predict what you think you will hear.

2 (62) Listen and complete these statements.

a Lima is also known as the City of ....Kings........ .
b The Spanish founded the city in ....
c There were around .... Inca temples and palaces when the Spanish arrived.
d Plaza Mayor is the .... in Lima.
e Lima was founded nearly .... years ago.
f In 1746 an .... destroyed almost all the city.

3 (62) Try to remember the answers to these questions. Then listen again and check.

a For how many years was Peru a colony of Spain?
   Almost 300 years..
b Who was Francisco Pizarro?
   ----
c In which building does the President of Peru live?
   ----
d How many buildings survived the disaster of 1746?
   ----
e What is the oldest building in Plaza Mayor?

Sound smart
Linking consonant–vowel

1 (63) If a word ends in a consonant, and the next word begins in a vowel, then the consonant sound moves to the beginning of the next word. For example, *get up*, *stop over*. Listen to these examples.

He told us a bit about when the Spanish arrived in Peru. An earthquake destroyed almost all of the city.

2 Look at these sentences and underline the sounds that are joined together.
   a Can I take a brochure, please?
   b We got on the boat and sailed across to the island.
   c I want a table with a view of the sea, if possible.
   d I had a good look around the castle.
   e We went out with a group of friends that afternoon.

3 (64) Listen and check. Then listen again and repeat.

E Speaking – Asking questions

Speaking strategy: Interrupting politely

1 In an informal talk it is usually possible to interrupt the speaker and ask a question. Here are some expressions you can use.

Sorry, can I ask a question? ☐
I'm sorry, but could I ask a question? ☐
Excuse me. I have a question. ☐
Sorry to interrupt, but … ☐
Could I interrupt for a moment? ☐

2 (62) Listen again to the talk. Tick ✓ the expressions you hear.

Speak up!

3 (65) Imagine you are on the same guided tour. You also want to interrupt to ask a question. Listen and ask to interrupt each time you hear a beep.

Example: a
You hear: It was the Spanish who actually founded the city of Lima. [beep]
You say: Sorry, can I ask a question?
You hear: Of course, go ahead.

F Speaking – Requesting more information

Speaking strategy: Asking for further details

1 **Look at this extract from the guided tour. Underline the expression the tourist uses to ask for further details.**

Tourist: Sorry, can I ask a question?
Guide: Yes.
Tourist: What about the Incas? They were here before the Spanish, weren't they? Could you tell us a bit more about them?

2 **Here are some more expressions you can use to ask for further information.**

Can you say (a bit) more about …?
I'd like to know more about …
I'd be interested to hear more about …

Speak up!

3 🎧66 **Imagine you are on a guided tour. Look at the information below. Listen and each time you hear a beep interrupt politely and ask for further details.**

Example: a
You hear: That's the Modern Art Museum, the most popular one in the city, and on the left … [beep]
You say: Sorry, can I ask a question? I'd like to know more about the museum. What is there to see?

a   museum
b   Mardi Gras
c   Lord Byron
d   castle
e   the National Palace

Can-do checklist

Tick what you can do.

	Can do	Need more practice
I can ask for recommendations before going on a trip.		
I can understand the details of a guided tour.		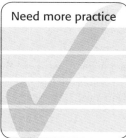
I can interrupt politely to ask for further explanation.		
I can ask for further details.		

Section 1

⊙ 67 Listen and reply to each statement you hear. Circle your answer.

Example:
You hear: What's up?
ⓐ Nothing much.
b Not at all.
c Yes, that's right.

1
a Not really.
b Me neither.
c So do I.

2
a Yes, I booked a table for eight o'clock.
b No, thank you. I'm full.
c It was lovely, thank you.

3
a That's too bad.
b Let's split it.
c Is that your best price?

4
a OK, I won't.
b Is that the best you can do?
c Yes, I do.

5
a How are you doing?
b OK. See you later.
c Me neither.

6
a Yes, I think so too.
b Yes, it is.
c Not much.

7
a Yes, it is.
b I'm not sure I agree.
c Would you? OK then.

8
a It's well worth the visit.
b It's a deal.
c Oh, good!

9
a Not really.
b Yes, it is.
c Why don't you?

10
a Yes, it is.
b I have a cough.
c No, that's fine.

Section 2

⊙ 68 Read each situation. Then listen and write the letter.

Example:
A friend tells you about a bargain he got recently. What do you say?
You hear:
a That's a great idea.
b That sounds good.
c Thanks for the tip.
You write: b

1 You're in a restaurant. You've been waiting for your drinks for half an hour. What do you say? ....

2 The printer you bought last week has broken. You take it back to the shop. What do you say? ....

3 Your friend offers you his old computer for £20. It's a good price. What do you say? ....

4 You have a very bad cold and call your boss to ask for the day off. What do you say? ....

5 You tell a friend about your wonderful holiday in Canada. What do you say? ....

6 The phone company tell you they can't repair your phone for another week. What do you say? ....

7 You're on a tour and want more details of a museum the guide mentioned. What do you say? ....

8 You are saying goodbye to a friend. What do you say? ....

9 A friend tells you they are very ill. What do you say? ....

10 You are sightseeing and want to ask about the local tourist bus. What do you say? ....

Section 3

Read each situation and (circle) your answer.

Example:
An estate agent shows you a house. It's nice, but expensive. How can you politely ask about an alternative?
ⓐ Do you have anything a little cheaper?
b It's too expensive. Show me something else.
c Is this all you have?

1 Which is the most effective way to maintain a conversation?
   a Smile and look friendly.
   b Ask lots of follow-up questions.
   c Talk as much as you can.

2 What should you do if you can't understand someone's accent?
   a Relax and try to 'tune in'.
   b Try to avoid speaking to them.
   c Smile and pretend to understand.

3 Which of these phrases can you use to make your point more forcefully?
   a Is it OK if …?
   b Do you think you could …?
   c I really must insist that …

4 To ask a question using a question tag, your voice should …
   a go down at the end of the sentence.
   b go up at the end of the sentence.
   c stay the same level.

5 The person you are speaking to is talking too quickly. What is the best thing to do?
   a Nothing. It would be rude to interrupt.
   b Say 'Slow down, can you?'
   c Say 'Please could you slow down a bit?'

6 Which of these things should you not do before you listen to a talk?
   a Ask yourself what you know about the topic.
   b Predict what you think you will hear.
   c Get a dictionary in case there are words you don't know.

7 You and your friend have had a meal and you want to share the bill. What do you say?
   a Shall we split the bill?
   b I'll get it.
   c It's my treat.

8 A window in your rented flat is broken. What's the best thing to say to the landlord?
   a You can repair the window, can't you?
   b Could you send someone to fix the window?
   c I think the window needs repairing.

9 Which of these is not a way to agree with someone?
   a Me neither.
   b I can't agree.
   c I couldn't agree more.

10 When you are speaking to someone, what should you do if you are not sure how to say something?
   a Check in a dictionary.
   b Keep talking and try to make yourself understood.
   c Stop talking and think about what to say.

Section 4

Read each statement and write your reply.

Example:
Is everything all right with your steak?
No, I'm afraid it's a little under-done.

1 If you ask me, people work harder these days than in the past.
   ----

2 What was the food like in the restaurant you went to last night?
   ----

3 The doctor said I have high blood pressure.
   ----

4 This watch costs £499. It's a bargain.
   ----

5 What are the symptoms?
   ----

6 So what was Paris like?
   ----

7 Let me get this, will you?
   ----

8 Can you recommend a good place to stay?
   ----

9 The shoes are faulty, but we can't accept responsibility.
   ----

10 Have you been taking anything for it?

Complete the phrases with *for*, *of* or *with*.
a work ....for.... a big company ☐
b be in charge .... overseas projects ☐
c be head .... a big department ☐
d be responsible .... making important decisions ☐
e deal ....complaints and queries ☐

Now tick ✓ the things you would like to do.

Match each verb with a phrase.
a solve — a file by mistake
b connect to — a faulty telephone
c arrange — the Internet
d delete — a problem
e repair — a meeting

go to Useful language p. 81

A Listening – Asking for services

1 💿2 Vicky works at a small marketing agency in Florida, US. There is a problem with the office photocopier, so she phones a local office supplies company. Listen and answer the questions.

a Is the photocopier still under guarantee?
   Yes, it has two years left on its guarantee.
b When did Kelta & Co buy it?
   ----
c What exactly is wrong with the photocopier?
   ----
d Has Vicky tried to fix it herself?
   ----
e When is she told someone can come to fix it?
   ----
f What time does she finally agree?

2 Tick ✓ how you would describe the attitude of the assistant Vicky speaks to.

helpful ☐
professional ☐
unfriendly ☐
uncooperative ☐

3 How satisfied is Vicky with the service she receives. Tick ✓ your answer.

very satisfied ☐
quite satisfied ☐
not very satisfied ☐
very dissatisfied ☐

Learning tip

When you are listening to someone, try to notice the speaker's tone of voice. The way the speaker sounds can tell you a lot about their attitude.

B Speaking – Making appointments

Speaking strategy: Fixing a time

1 Look at these expressions you can use when making an appointment.

What time day date	would be most convenient? would suit you best? is good for you?	
Sometime Any time	this morning early next week after three between 10.30 and 12	would be great. is OK for me. would be fine.
What / How about … Shall we say …	tomorrow afternoon? the 24th?	

2 **Listen again to Vicky's conversation. <u>Underline</u> the expression in Exercise 1 you hear.**

Speak up!

3 Imagine you want to make some appointments. Use the ideas below to fix a time.

Example: a
You say: How about Monday? Any time in the afternoon would be fine.

a Monday / afternoon
b Friday / 2pm–4pm
c Tuesday / not before 10am
d Friday morning / 10am
e early next week / before Thursday

4 **Now listen and respond to each person, fixing a time.**

Example: a
You hear: We have the books you ordered. When would be a good time to drop them round?
You say: Shall we say two o'clock tomorrow afternoon?

a 2pm tomorrow   d 11am–1pm
b Thursday morning   e Tuesday 19th, in the afternoon
c Friday morning   f between three and four

C Speaking – Getting what you want

Speaking strategy: Insisting

1 Look at this extract. What phrase does Vicky use to insist on an earlier time?

Assistant: We can't get anyone there until late afternoon, I'm afraid.
Vicky: I'm sorry, but that's no good at all. We're very busy here and we need this fixing immediately.

2 Here are some more expressions you can use when you need to be forceful.

It's simply not acceptable to …
You have to do something …
You can't expect me to …
I really must instist that …

Speak up!

3 **Imagine you work for a large company. You experience the following problems and call the maintenance department. Listen and respond, insisting on your point.**

Example: a
You hear: I'm sorry. We won't be able to repair it for at least four weeks.
You say: But you can't expect me to use this computer for the next four weeks. I can't get any work done. I need it fixing as soon as possible.

a Your computer keeps crashing.
b The smoke alarm in your office is faulty. It constantly turns on and off, and disrupts everyone.
c You have been waiting for five weeks for a new light in your office.
d You are too cold in your office and want a new heater.
e You have a lot of heavy boxes to take to reception for collection by a courier company in 20 minutes.
f The toilet in your department has been out of order for nearly a month. It's a five-minute walk to the next one. You've noticed staff productivity is falling as a result of the time lost.

D Listening – A hard sell

Did you know ...?

Hard sell is an aggressive way of selling that puts pressure on the buyer. *Soft sell* is a more indirect technique that aims to influence the buyer's emotions. One survey of internet advertizing showed that hard sell techniques are popular in the US, while the soft sell approach is favoured in Japan.

1 🔴⑤ Stuart Hawthorne is a salesman in Adelaide, Australia. He's visiting Melanie Clark, a potential customer at a large insurance company. Listen and answer the questions.

a What do you think Stuart is trying to sell?

----

b Tick ✓ how you would describe Stuart's manner.
friendly and flexible ☐   confident and relaxed ☐
rude and aggressive ☐   direct and rather pushy ☐

c Tick ✓ how you think Melanie feels.
offended ☐   pressurized ☐
amused ☐   impressed ☐

2 🔴⑤ Now listen again and write your answers to these questions.

a What are the benefits of the Gold Plan?

----

b How many computers will be covered by the plan?

----

c What extra incentive does Stuart offer?

Focus on ...
conditionals

Complete the sentences using the first conditional form of the verbs in brackets.

a If you ___order___ (order) now, I ʼll give (give) you ten percent off.

b You _____ (have) it next Monday if you _____ (pay) today.

c If you _____ (not / decide) now, it _____ (be) too late.

d We _____ (not / buy) it if the price _____ (not / be) right.

e _____ (you / call) again next week if you _____ (have) time?

f If you _____ (pay) cash, we _____ (not / charge) for delivery.

Choose the correct time clause to complete each sentence.

a I won't agree *unless* / *when* you promise to deliver by Friday.

b *As long as* / *Until* you offer me more money, I'll do it.

c I'll sign the contract *after* / *until* I see you.

d *When* / *Until* the board agrees, we will make the decision.

e I'll leave the company *unless* / *if* there's no hope of promotion.

f I won't call you again *unless* / *until* Friday morning.

Class bonus

Half the class are buyers; half the class are sellers.

Buyers: Imagine you want to buy some new office equipment. Decide what you want. Then shop around and use your negotiating skills to get the best deal, e.g. a discount, free delivery.

Sellers: You have an office supplies company. Make a list of items you sell. Then try to sell as many as you can. Use hard and soft sell techniques. Try to negotiate the best deal for each item.

E Speaking – Negotiating

Speaking strategy: Bargaining

1 Look at this extract from Stuart and Melanie's conversation.

If you agree now, I'll give you a five percent discount.

2 🔘6 Look at these expressions. Listen and repeat.

Is that your best offer?
You'll have to do better than that, I'm afraid.
If you order now, we'll give you a discount.
We might be able to come down on price if you order in bulk.
I'll give ten percent extra free, provided that you sign a one-year contract.

3 Which expressions would you use:

a to ask for a better deal?

----

b to offer a better deal?

Speak up!

4 Imagine you are a sales person. Use the expressions above to offer the following incentives.

Example: a
You say: If you order now, I'll give you an eight percent reduction.

a order now / an eight percent reduction
b pay in advance / free delivery
c free installation / order two
d one-year free insurance / order in bulk
e 25% discount / sign a two-year contract

Sound smart
Using stress for emphasis

1 🔘7 We usually stress the important words in a sentence. Listen to this example.
   A: OK, so if I pay in advance, you'll give me a ten percent discount?
   B: Yes, and if you pay **now**, then I'll give you a **fifteen** percent discount.

2 Look at these conversations and underline where you think the greatest stress will be.
   a A: If we agree to the deal, we will lose control of the company.
      B: Yes, but if we don't agree to the deal, the company will collapse.
   b A: If we increase our prices, we will make more profit.
      B: Yes, but if we decrease our prices, we will get more customers.
   c A: If we move production to Asia, costs will go down.
      B: Yes, and if we don't move production to Asia, we will be uncompetitive.

3 🔘8 Listen and check. Then listen again and repeat, emphasizing the important information.

E X tra practice

Go to the BBC Learning English website and type 'negotiating a contract listen' in the search box. Press enter and then choose a link that interests you. Complete any exercises.
http://www.bbc.co.uk/worldservice/learningenglish/

Can-do checklist

Tick what you can do.

	Can do	Need more practice
I can make an appointment at a time that is convenient for me.	✔	✔
I can insist on what I want politely but firmly.	✔	✔
I can try to bargain and negotiate.		

Get ready to listen and speak

Write the number of each item (1–7) next to the correct word or phrase (a–g).

a a chequebook   _2_
b a bank card   ......
c a bank book   ......
d a bank statement   ......
e a paying-in slip   ......
f an ATM machine   ......
g some traveller's cheques ......

go to Useful language p. 81

A Listening – At a bank

1 🔊 9 **Listen to ten office workers in London ask for services at a bank. What does each person want to do? Complete the notes.**

a open an _account_
b order a new ....
c check his ....
d pay a cheque into her ....
e send some money ....
f deposit money into his ....
g pay his electricity ....
h buy some ....
i arrange an ....
j order a new ....

2 🔊 10 **Now listen to four replies. Match each reply (1–4) with one of the services requested above.**

   1 [a]   2 ☐   3 ☐   4 ☐

3 🔊 10 **Listen again to each reply. Make notes of all the important information.**

1 *Need ID (passport / driving licence),*

2

3

4

Learning tip

Taking notes helps to focus your attention. Don't try to write everything you hear – just concentrate on the most important information. Note only the key words and ignore everything else.

Focus on ...
money

Match each verb with an expression.
a borrow   an overdraft
b lend   a cheque into your account
c withdraw   money to someone
d deposit   money from your account
e arrange   money from the bank

Complete with the missing prepositions.
a save ....up.... to buy something
b pay .... a cheque
c take .... a loan
d fill .... an application form
e apply .... a mortgage
f invest .... a company

Did you know ...?

In British English, many people say *quid* rather than *pound.* (*Can you lend me 20 quid?*) In American English, people say *buck* rather than *dollar*, and in Canada, a *dollar* is also called a *loonie.*

B Listening – Understanding details

1 🔘**11** Raymond, from Hong Kong, is working in Canada and decides to open a savings account. Listen to a bank clerk explain various savings accounts. Tick ✓ the account Raymond chooses.

First Reserve ☐   Bonus Saver ☐   Regular Saver ☐   e-Savings ☐

2 🔘**11** Listen again and find six mistakes in the form below.

Type of savings account	Interest rate	When interest is paid	Conditions
First Reserve	2.5% 3.5%	annually	at least $15,000
Bonus Saver	3%	every three months	20 days' notice before withdrawal
Regular Saver	2.3%	every two months	no interest paid if withdraw money
e-Savings	4.5%	every month	save at least $100 per month

C Speaking – Confirming details

Speaking strategy: Making sure you understand

1 <u>Underline</u> the phrase Raymond uses to make sure he has understood correctly.

Bank clerk: Our e-Savings account is instant access, too.
Raymond: Does that mean I can get at the money immediately?
Bank clerk: Yes, and there's no penalty.

2 **Here are some other expressions you can use.**

So, in other words, ...?   Do you mean ...?
So you're saying that ...?   So that means ...?

Speak up!

3 🔘**12** You will hear five statements. Use the expressions in Exercises 1 and 2 to reply to each statement, confirming the details.

Example: a
You hear: The interest rate is 3% but, if you have over ₤25,000 invested, then it goes up to 3.5%.
You say: So that means if I save over ₤25,000, I'll get 3.5% interest?

D Speaking – Asking about terms you don't understand

Speaking strategy: Asking for clarification

1 Look at this extract. <u>Underline</u> the phrase Raymond uses to ask the bank clerk to explain a term he doesn't understand.

Bank clerk: There's a penalty if you take money out.
Raymond: What do you mean by 'penalty'?
Bank clerk: Well, if you withdraw money, then you won't get any interest for that month.

2 Here are some other expressions you can use.

What exactly does … mean?
I'm sorry. Can you explain what … means?

Speak up!

3 🔘**13** You will hear five statements. Use the expressions above to ask about the words you don't understand.

Example: a
You hear: This account has a variable rate of interest.
You say: I'm sorry. Can you explain what 'variable' means?
You hear: Variable means the interest rate can go down or up.

a variable?   c minimum balance?   e automatic fee-free overdraft?
b secured?   d lump sum?

Focus on ... conditionals

Complete the sentences, using the expressions below.

~~you want~~	you will get
you open	~~you should give~~
you take	unless you have
you won't get	you aren't

a If ___you want___ to withdraw some money, then ___you should give___ 30 days' notice.
b If _____ money out, _____ any interest for that month.
c You can't open a First Reserve account _____ £5,000 to invest.
d If _____ a Bonus Saver account, _____ an interest rate of three percent.
e If _____ online, then you can't have an e-Savings account.

E Listening – In a post office

1 🔘**14** Listen to eight customers ask for services at a post office. Tick ✓ the services they ask for.

pay utility bills ☐
exchange currency ☐
buy car insurance ☐
transfer money ☐
save and invest money ☐
top up your mobile phone ☐
get a personal loan ☐
get a credit card ☐

apply for a driving licence ☐
buy travel insurance ☐
apply for or renew a passport ☐
buy phone cards ☐
redirect post ☐
collect their pension ☐
buy home insurance ☐

2 🔘**15** Brigitte is in a post office in London. She wants to send a package. Listen and answer the questions.

a Where does she want to send the package?
   To Switzerland.
b Who is she sending it to?
   _____
c Why does she have to fill in a Customs label?
   _____
d What service does she decide to use?
   Surface mail ☐   Airmail ☐
   International Signed For ☐   Airsure ☐

3 🔘**15** Listen again and complete the Customs label.

CUSTOMS DECLARATION DÉCLARATION EN DOUANE		CN 22 May be opened officially Peut être ouvert d'office
Great Britain\Grande-Bretagne	**Important!**	See instructions on the back

	Gift\Cadeau		Commercial sample\Echantillon commercial
	Documents		Other\Autre *Tick one or more boxes*

Quantity and detailed description of contents (1) Quantité et description détaillée du contenu	Weight (*in kg*)(2) Poids	Value (3) Valeur
_____	____	____
_____	____	____
_____	____	____

For commercial items only If known, HS tariff number (4) and country of origin of goods (5) N°tarifaire du SH et pays d'origine des marchandises (si connus) HS238 UK	Total Weight Poids total (*in kg*) (6)	Total Value (7) Valeur totale

I, the undersigned, whose name and address are given on the item, certify that the particulars given in this declaration are correct and that this item does not contain any dangerous article or articles prohibited by legislation or by postal or customs regulations

Date and sender's signature (8)   *Brigitte Tenkhoff*   *July 3rd '20.*

4 🔵15 Try to remember the missing information in the chart. Then listen again and check.

	Time	Cost
Surface mail	a _two weeks_	£b _____
Airmail	c _____	£d _____
International Signed For	three days	£e _____
Airsure	f _____	£g _____

Sound smart
Corrective stress

1 🔵16 Listen and notice how B gives extra emphasis to the correct information.
A: OK, so if I send this by International Signed For, it'll get there in two days?
B: No, it'll get there in <u>three</u> days. If you send it by <u>Airsure</u>, it'll get there in <u>two</u> days.

2 Look at these dialogues and underline where you think the corrective stress will be.
a A: So I have to fill in a CN22 Customs label?
B: No, you need to fill in a CN23 Customs label.
b A: So I fill in a VN1 form and then go to the Payment section?
B: No, go to the Payment section first and then you can fill in a VN1.
c A: Did you say it will take two weeks by standard mail?
B: No, it'll take three weeks by standard mail. It'll take two weeks if you send it Swiftmail.

3 🔵17 Listen and check. Then listen again and try to speak at the same time as the customer.

E X tra practice

Take a look at the websites below for more information on the services offered by post offices around the world. Take notes of any useful information and then imagine you are telling a friend about what you discovered. If possible, record what you say and listen to yourself afterwards.
http://www.usps.com/ (the United States)
http://www.royalmail.com/ (the UK)
http://www.canadapost.ca/ (Canada)
http://www.auspost.com.au/ (Australia)
http://www.sapo.co.za/ (South Africa)

Class bonus

With your partner, role play two conversations: one in a bank and another in a post office.
In a bank
Customer: You want to find out about business savings accounts.
Clerk: Answer your customer's questions in detail.
In a post office
Customer: You want to send some company brochures and advertizing material.
Clerk: Explain the mail services available and any differences between them.
When you finish each conversation, swap roles and try again.

Can-do checklist

Tick what you can do.

	Can do	Need more practice
I can ask for a wide range of services at banks and post offices.		
I can understand detailed explanations of different bank accounts.		
I can ask about and understand various ways of sending mail abroad.		
I can ask for clarification and explanation where necessary.		

Unit 11
My bag's been stolen

go to Useful language p. 82

- Which emergency services have you had experience of?
  police ☐   fire department ☐
  ambulance ☐   coastguard ☐

- How many phrases can you make by adding *police* or *fire* to the words below?
  officer   car   brigade   fighter   alarm
  engine   station   siren   force

  police officer, _____
  _____

- Unscramble the letters to find the verbs and complete each expression.
  a orretp   ___report___ an accident
  b nweisst   _____ a crime
  c mcitmo   _____ a crime
  d earkb   _____ the law
  e ctcah   _____ a criminal
  f tiingavtese   _____ a robbery
  g aepesc   _____ from the police
  h reasrt   _____ a suspect
  i crgaeh   _____ someone with a crime

A Listening – Reporting a crime

1 Wen Ling, a Chinese student in the UK, reports a crime at the campus security office. Look at the form and identify the information to listen for.

Learning tip

Whenever possible, try to identify the information you need *before* you listen. That way you are better prepared. Then, while you listen, focus only on listening for those details and don't worry about anything else.

Bristol City University

Crime report form

Day / time: ᵃ___Tuesday___ / ᵇ_____

Type of crime: ᶜ☐ theft   ☐ burglary
                ☐ assault ☐ other: _____

Location: ᵈ_____

Victim: Name: ᵉ_____
        Address: ᶠ_____

Details of crime: ᵍ_____

Suspect: Appearance: ʰ_____
_____
_____

Additional details: ⁱ_____
_____

Focus on ...
adjectives to describe appearance

Write these words and expressions next to the correct category.

in his thirties	straight	casual	stocky
wavy	slim	permed	oval
muscular	curly	forty-ish	skinny
round	scruffy	overweight	square
shoulder-length	smart		

Height / build: _____
Hair: _____
Age: _in his thirties_____
Face: _____
Style of dress: _____

2 🔘18 Now listen and complete the form.

B Speaking – Giving descriptions (1)

Speaking strategy: Describing someone's appearance

1 Look at this extract. <u>Underline</u> the words and phrases Wen Ling uses to describe the thief.

Guard: OK. Did you get a look at him?

Wen Ling: Yes. He was medium height with short dark hair and glasses. Oh, and he had a moustache.

Speak up!

2 Look at these people. Describe each person's appearance in detail, including what they are wearing.

C Speaking – Giving descriptions (2)

Speaking strategy: Describing things

1 Look at this extract. <u>Underline</u> the words and phrases Wen Ling uses to describe her bag.

Guard: Can you describe the bag?

Wen Ling: It's a small, black leather bag, with a zip along the top and a shoulder strap.

Speak up!

2 Look at these bags and describe each one as fully as you can.

Example: a

You say: It's a small, black leather bag, with a zip along the top and a shoulder strap.

Focus on ...
order of adjectives

Look at the usual order of adjectives below, and then rearrange the adjectives in each sentence.

opinion – size – age – shape – colour – origin – material

a I lost a *Italian blue lovely silk* scarf yesterday.
  I lost a _____lovely blue Italian silk_____ scarf yesterday.
b Someone's stolen my *black new denim* jacket.
  Someone's stolen my _____ jacket.
c My *pink wonderful diamond* bracelet is missing.
  My _____ bracelet is missing.
d It's a *rectangular large mahogany* desk.
  It's a _____ desk.
e Someone's taken my *French tall crystal* vase.
  Someone's taken my _____ vase.

Class bonus

Imagine someone has stolen something of yours, e.g. your camera or mobile phone. With your partner, role play a conversation to report the theft.

D Listening – Calling the emergency services

1 🔘 **19** Hassan, from Syria, works in the north of England. He is on his way home when he sees a traffic accident. He calls 999 to tell the emergency services. Listen and tick ✓ the picture that best describes the scene.

a ☐

b ☐

c ☐

2 🔘 **19** Can you remember the order the operators asked these questions? Number each question 1–4. Then listen again and check.

Where do you need the ambulance to come to? ☐
Which service do you require? ☐ 1 ☐
What's happened? ☐
How many people are hurt? ☐

3 🔘 **19** Listen again and write the answer to each question.

1 ....
2 ....
3 ....
4 ....

Did you know …?

Different countries have different numbers for the emergency services.

UK 999
US 911
Australia 000
New Zealand 111
South Africa 112

E Speaking – Reporting an emergency

Speaking strategy: Getting to the point

1 If you need to call the emergency services, you should speak clearly and answer each question as directly as you can. You need to:

1 ask for the service you require
2 say where you are
3 say what has happened
4 say if any people are injured.

Speak up!

2 🔘 **20** Imagine you witness the following situations and call the emergency services. Listen and answer each question as directly as you can.

a You are waiting at Richmond bus station when an elderly lady next to you falls to the ground unconscious.
b You are walking past Highcroft School one evening when you see a fire in an upstairs window.

F Listening – Giving a statement to the police

1 🔊 **21** Listen to Hassan describe what he saw to a police officer. Choose the correct location of the accident on the map: A, B, C or D.

2 🔊 **22** Look at the statements below. Then listen to the rest of the conversation and tick ✓ True or False for each statement.

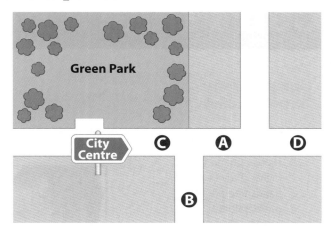

		True	False
a	The car was speeding.	☐	✓
b	The cyclist was in the middle of the road.	☐	☐
c	The cyclist had no lights on his bike.	☐	☐
d	The car was on the wrong side of the road.	☐	☐
e	The accident happened close to Hassan.	☐	☐
f	Hassan helped the injured men before calling 999.	☐	☐

Sound smart
The schwa /ə/

1 🔊 **23** Listen to this sentence and notice the schwa /ə/.
I w<u>a</u>s walking past th<u>e</u> park, heading t<u>o</u>wards th<u>e</u> city centr<u>e</u>.

2 Now look at these sentences and <u>underline</u> every schwa.
   a How fast was the car travelling?
   b So the collision happened here, you say?
   c There was a big crash and then silence.

3 🔊 **24** Listen and check. Then listen again and repeat each sentence. Try to pronounce the schwa sound each time.

Class bonus

Make a group and role play the situation.
Police officer: Interview everybody. Decide who is to blame for the accident.
Witnesses: Say exactly what you saw.
Cyclist: Give your side of the story.
Motorist: Give your version of events.

E✗tra practice

Watch these short road safety TV and cinema adverts made by the UK Department of Transport.
http://www.thinkroadsafety.gov.uk/campaigns/general/generalmedia.htm#video

Can-do checklist

Tick what you can do.

	Can do	Need more practice
I can report a crime and give exact details of people and objects.		
I can report an incident to the emergency services.		
I can get straight to the point.		

Unit 12
Can I take a message?

go to Useful language p. 82

Get ready to listen and speak

○ Match each type of phone (a–f) with a picture (1–6).
a corded phone 3
b mobile phone ☐
c digital cordless phone ☐
d hands-free phone ☐
e public phone ☐
f satellite phone ☐

1

2

3

4

5

6

A Listening – Taking a message

1 🔊25 **Listen to Kieran, a personal assistant, take a telephone message. What does the caller want to do?**

Set up a meeting ☐
Change some arrangements ☐
Complain about a problem ☐

2 🔊25 **Listen again and complete the message.**

Ivro Industries

While you were out

Name: ª Kenji Fujita

Contact details: ᵇ

Message: ᶜ

B Speaking – Getting it right

Speaking strategy: Repeating key information

1 Look at this extract. Notice how Kieran repeats only the key information.

> Kieran: OK, so … meet in your office in Building 3, not the main building, at four o'clock, not two. Got it.

2 Here are some expressions you can use to notify the caller you are going to review their message.

> OK, so …
> Right. I think I've got that.
> Let me repeat that, just to make sure.
> I'll just go over that to confirm.

Speak up!

3 🔊26 Imagine you are a personal assistant. While your boss is out of the office, five people call and ask you to take a message. Listen and repeat the key information.

> Example: a
> You hear: Can you say that I'll be about thirty minutes late? If she wants to start the meeting without me, that's fine, because I can't guarantee exactly when I'll be there. The traffic's terrible.
> You say: OK, so you'll be about thirty minutes late and it's OK for the meeting to start without you.

Focus on …
telephoning

Choose one word to complete each sentence.

call	~~hang~~	hold	get	put	give	hear

a Please don't _____hang_____ up.
b I'll just put you on _____ .
c Can I _____ you back later?
d Can you _____ me through?
e When shall I _____ you a ring?
f It's great to _____ from you.
g I always _____ the engaged signal.

Match the words and phrases that mean the same.

American English	British English
1 to call collect	a engaged
2 cell	b phone box
3 toll-free	c to reverse the charges
4 busy	d freephone
5 call box	e mobile

Learning tip

When you take a message, it is a good idea to repeat the important information back to the caller to make sure you have understood correctly. This also gives the caller an opportunity to confirm all the details are correct. Just summarize the important points. There is no need to repeat the message word for word.

C Speaking – Making sure you have understood

Speaking strategy: Asking for clarification

1 Look at the phrases below you can use to ask a caller for clarification.

> Sorry. What was that last part again, please?
> Is that spelled …?
> Did you say …?
> You said …, right?

2 🔊25 Listen to Kieran and Kenji's conversation once more and tick ✓ the phrases Kieran uses.

Speak up!

3 🔊27 Listen to each person leave a message and ask for clarification to check you have understood.

> Example: a
> You hear: Yes, please. Tell her Mr MacGregor called, would you?
> You say: Is that spelled M-A-C-G-R-E-G-O-R?

D Listening – Note taking

28 Now listen to Kieran take quite a long and detailed message. Complete his notes.

Hilda ª ____Birghard____

Queries for ᵇ _____

1 What percentage of clients are
  ᶜ _____ (i.e. have
  ᵈ _____ before)?
  + what is their ᵉ _____ ?

2 How many sales from ᶠ _____ ?
  + what was the ᵍ _____
  compared to ʰ _____ ?

Did you know …?

Research shows that seven out of ten callers choose to hang up rather than leave a message on an answerphone.

Class bonus

1 Imagine you are at work and you need to call a colleague. Decide who you want to call, and why.
2 Find a partner and sit back-to-back. Role play your conversation, leaving a message. Your partner should take notes.

E Listening – Leaving a message

1 **29** Listen and complete these expressions.

a Could I ____leave a message____ , please?
b Thanks a lot. I _____ .
c Does that _____ ?
d Do you think you could _____ ?
e Can I ask _____ ?
f Have you _____ ?
g _____ , please?
h _____ taking a message?
i I _____ . Thank you.
j Sorry. I didn't _____ .
k Could you _____ ?

2 Which expressions can you use:
  to ask to leave a message? _a_
  to thank the person taking the message? _____
  to check the person has understood you correctly? _____

3 Which expressions might you hear if the person taking the message wants to know your name?

  _____

4 **28** Listen again to Kieran and Hilda's conversation. Tick ✓ the expressions in Exercise 1 (a–k) you hear.

Learning tip

Before making an important call, make a note of what you want to say. Then if you need to leave a message, you will be sure not to forget anything.

F Speaking – Leaving a voicemail message

Speaking strategy: Leaving effective messages

1 Read these things you should do when you leave a voicemail message. Number each step in order (1–5).

Say what action is necessary ☐
Give the reason for your call ☐
Finish the call ☐
Give your contact details, if necessary ☐
Give your name (and company, if necessary) 1

2 For each step, write some phrases you can use.

Example: 1
You say: Hi. This is ... / It's ... calling.

Speak up!

3 Imagine you call an important client and get put through to their voicemail. Use this information to leave a message.

Sam Kershaw / Industrial Design / your order is ready / need to pay in full before can send / call Accounts to pay / ring me if necessary / office 0208-451-5690
mobile 07967-431094

E✗tra practice

Find some friends who want to practise their English. Agree that when you call each other you will speak in English. Call each other and, when necessary, leave messages. Try to continue practising in this way and make it a regular habit.

Sound smart
Connected speech

1 🔘 30 In spoken English, sounds are often shortened, missed out or joined together. Listen to this sentence. There are eight words, but they are spoken in just three sections.

Do you think you could take a message?
/djəθɪŋk/ /juːkʊdteɪ/ /kəmesɪdʒ/

2 🔘 31 Listen to these sentences and count the number of words. Contractions, e.g. *I'd*, count as two words (*I would*).
a Would you mind taking a message, please? ..7..
b ......
c ......
d ......
e ......

3 🔘 31 Listen again and repeat.

Class bonus

1 Imagine you and your classmates work together in the same company. Decide who you want to call, and why.
2 Call a classmate on their mobile phone and leave a voicemail message. Give your name, say why you are calling, say what you want them to do, give your contact details and then finish the call.
3 Check any messages on your mobile phone. Then call back to give your reply.

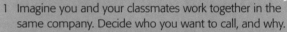

Can-do checklist

Tick what you can do.

	Can do	Need more practice
I can note all the important details in a complex phone message.		
I can ask for clarification and check I have understood.		
I can leave a message and check others have understood me.		
I can leave a clear and concise voicemail message.		

Unit 13
Let's get started

go to Useful language p. 82

Get ready to listen and speak

○ Match words with a similar meaning.
- a iron out — private
- b absent — achieve
- c confidential — suspend
- d adjourn — not present
- e accomplish — resolve

○ Complete each sentence with a word.

minutes	show	compulsory	~~vote~~	chair	agenda	motion	objectives

- a Let's take a ......vote...... .
- b Mrs Kendry is .... for this meeting.
- c What's on the .... ?
- d Who's going to take the .... ?
- e Attendance is ....
- f The .... was passed unanimously.
- g What are the .... of this meeting?
- h It was decided by a .... of hands.

A Listening – The language of meetings

1 ●32 **Listen to five sentences and tick ✓ which sentence you hear.**
- a I think so too. ✓   I think that's true. ☐
- b Do you agree? ☐   Do you see? ☐
- c Could you say what you mean? ☐
   Could you explain what you mean? ☐
- d Let's move on, shall we? ☐
   Let's move on, can we? ☐
- e It's not ideal. ☐   It's a deal. ☐
- f Yes, I agree. ☐   Yes, I see. ☐

2 ●33 **Listen to eight sentences and count the number of words in each one.**
a ⑥ b ☐ c ☐ d ☐ e ☐ f ☐ g ☐ h ☐

3 ●33 **Listen again and write each expression.**
- a *I think you're absolutely right.*
- b ....
- c ....
- d ....
- e ....
- f ....
- g ....
- h ....

4 ●33 **Now listen again and repeat each expression, using the same stress and rhythm.**

5 **Match each expression (a–h) with a function (1–8).**
- 1 Starting a meeting ☐
- 2 Asking for opinions ☐
- 3 Agreeing [a]
- 4 Moving forward ☐
- 5 Keeping to the point ☐
- 6 Asking for clarification ☐
- 7 Disagreeing ☐
- 8 Interrupting ☐

6 **Now look at these expressions. Write the number of each function (1–8) in Exercise 5 next to the correct expression.**

I think so too. ③
How do you feel about …? ☐
Right. Let's kick off with … ☐
Sorry, but I don't agree. ☐
I'm not sure that's relevant. ☐
OK. Let's go on to … ☐
What exactly do you mean? ☐
Can I say something at this point? ☐

Learning tip

When you are in a meeting, try to listen out for key expressions like these. They will help you understand what is going on and follow the discussion more closely.

B Listening – Participating in a discussion

1 🔘 **34 Listen to this extract from a company meeting and tick ✓ the phrases you hear.**

Could we perhaps …? ☐
What / How about …ing? ☐
We might consider …ing. ☐
I suggest we … ☐
I propose we … ☐
Why don't we …? ☐

2 🔘 **34 Listen again. Tick ✓ the suggestions each person accepts, and cross ✗ the suggestions they reject.**

Suggestions	Catherine	Mark	Julie	Peter
Spend more money on marketing	✗			
Hire a new sales manager				

Did you know …?

According to a report by *Industry Week*, 27% of workers feel that meetings are the biggest causes of wasted time at work.

C Speaking – Asking for opinions

Speaking strategy: Bringing someone into a discussion

1 🔘 **35 Listen and notice the way the speaker's voice goes up and down.**

I'd like to start by asking Celaya.

Carol, do you have any thoughts?

How do you feel about that, Miguel?

Perhaps you can give us your opinion, Mr Tanaka?

Mustafa, what's your reaction?

Jenny?

🔘 **35 Listen again and repeat each expression. Try to raise and lower your voice in the same way.**

2 🔘 **34 Listen again to the meeting.**

a Which of these ways of bringing someone into the discussion do you hear?

----

b Who do you think is the chair?

Speak up!

3 Imagine you are chairing a meeting. Bring the following people into the discussion, raising and lowering your voice appropriately.

Example: a
You say: I'd like to start by asking Vicky.

a Vicky
b Frances
c Mr Gonzales
d Martha
e Mrs Marsh

D Speaking – Responding to suggestions

Speaking strategy: Accepting and rejecting suggestions

1 Look at the expressions and decide if each one is used to either accept or reject a suggestion. Tick ✓ your answers.

	Accept	Reject
That's fair enough.	✓	☐
I'm not very keen on that idea (at all).	☐	☐
I don't see it like that at all.	☐	☐
I couldn't disagree more.	☐	☐
I think that's a good idea.	☐	☐
I'm afraid that's not how I see it.	☐	☐
I have no problem with that.	☐	☐
That sounds reasonable to me.	☐	☐

2 🔊34 Listen again to the meeting. Tick ✓ the expressions you hear.

Speak up!

3 🔊36 Imagine you are in a meeting. Listen to each suggestion and respond.

Example: a
You hear: Could we perhaps spend more money on marketing?
You say: No, I don't like that idea at all.

a Reject	c Reject	e Reject
b Accept	d Accept	f Accept

Sound smart
Intonation in questions

1 🔊37 Questions that have a *Yes / No* answer usually have rising intonation. Questions that begin *Wh-* usually have falling intonation. Listen and notice how the speaker's voice goes up and down in these questions.

Do you think we should go ahead?

Is everyone happy with that decision?

What do you think we should do?

Who's going to take responsibility for this?

2 🔊38 Look at these questions. Does the intonation go up or down at the end? Tick ✓ your answers. Then listen and check.

		↗	↘
a	Does everyone agree?	✓	☐
b	Is that your final answer?	☐	☐
c	Where are the sales figures?	☐	☐
d	Why are the results so poor?	☐	☐
e	Do you think the situation will improve?	☐	☐
f	Does this price include delivery?	☐	☐
g	Who's the new marketing manager?	☐	☐
h	Have you finished the report yet?	☐	☐

3 Now practise saying the questions with the correct intonation.

E Speaking – Clarifying what you mean

Speaking strategy: Correcting misunderstandings

1 Notice the expressions you can use to correct someone who has misunderstood you.

That's not quite what I meant.
Sorry. I think you've misunderstood me.
Sorry. What I meant was …
I don't think you understand what I mean.

Speak up!

2 🔊39 Imagine you are in a meeting. Someone has misunderstood you and you want to correct them. Listen and respond, correcting each person.

Example: a
You hear: So, I guess that means you're happy with the sales figures.
You say: That's not quite what I meant. I think the sales figures are poor, but they'll improve.

a figures are poor but they'll improve
b output will stay the same
c shouldn't launch later than February
d could have been better
e need time to think about it

F Listening – Finishing a meeting

1 🔊 **40** **Listen and complete the missing information in each summary.**

a   managers to get a _____ / sales force to _____

b   new product is _____ / some _____ and _____ issues

c   need to start a programme of _____ / begin next _____

2 🔊 **40** **Listen again and complete the expression each person uses to show they are going to give a summary.**

a   Let me _____

b   I'll quickly _____

c   To _____

3 🔊 **40** **Listen again and tick ✓ the expression you hear each person use to end the meeting.**

I think we've covered everything, so shall we call it a day? ☐

We'll have to cut this meeting short, I'm afraid. ☐

I'm afraid we've run out of time, so let's bring this to a close, shall we? ☐

It looks like we can finish early today. ☐

Did you know ...?

Thanks to high speed internet connectivity, 'videoconferencing' is becoming more popular. People don't have to spend time and money travelling to international meetings – they can speak via video link on their PC from anywhere in the world.

Class bonus

Imagine you work for a toy manufacturing company. You attend a meeting to discuss poor sales performance. Make a group and choose one person to chair the meeting. Role play the meeting.

Factors affecting sales:

–   Your biggest competitor has launched an advertizing campaign.

–   There are safety worries over your latest child's doll.

–   There were problems at the distribution centre.

–   New export taxes are putting off overseas buyers.

E X tra practice

Go to the *BBC Learning English* website and type 'meeting listen' in the search box. Press enter and then choose a link that interests you. Complete any exercises. www.bbc.co.uk/worldservice/learningenglish/

Can-do checklist

Tick what you can do.

	Can do	Need more practice
I can actively participate in meetings, bringing others into the discussion.		
I can make and accept or reject suggestions.		
I can clarify my viewpoint and correct misunderstandings.		
I can summarize the main points and bring a meeting to an end.		

Unit 14
Good morning, everyone

Get ready to listen and speak

○ Match each word (a–d) with a definition (1–4).
   a lecture [2] b tutorial [ ] c seminar [ ] d presentation [ ]

   1 a meeting where a group of students discuss a topic together with a teacher
   2 a formal talk given to a group of students by a professor or lecturer
   3 a one-to-one meeting between a student and a teacher
   4 a talk given by a student to the class

○ Have you ever been to a lecture in English?

○ Number these factors in order of importance (1 = quite important, 5 = extremely important).
A good lecture should:
...... be informative.
...... start and finish on time.
...... have time for questions.
...... be easy to understand.
...... be entertaining.

go to Useful language p. 83

A Listening – Understanding the main idea

🔊 **41** Listen to Dr Gandley speak to a group of new students at his Engineering Department. For each extract, tick ✓ the main point he is trying to make.

Extract 1
a It is unsafe to eat or drink in the lab. [ ]
b You should wear safety clothing at all times. [ ]
c You must always follow the safety rules. [ ]
d You should keep doors and windows closed. [ ]

Extract 2
a The college constantly updates its facilities. [ ]
b The resources and facilities of the college are excellent. [ ]
c Both lectures and project work are equally important. [ ]
d The college is proud of its history and achievements. [ ]

Extract 3
a Both theory and practical research are important. [ ]
b The area of sustainable energy is a particular interest. [ ]
c Engineering solutions provide the answer to climate change. [ ]
d The college aims to be the best in the world. [ ]

Learning tip

Remember that your aim when listening to a lecture is not to make a note of everything the lecturer says. Your goal is to understand the content of the lecture and the key points the lecturer is trying to make.

B Listening – Seeing the big picture

1 You are going to listen to an extract from a lecture called *Humans and the Planet*. Before you listen, underline the topics you think might be covered in the lecture.

education ☐   transport ☐   food ☐
languages ☐   the Internet ☐   carbon dioxide ☐
animals ☐   space ☐   sport ☐
crime ☐   the weather ☐   recycling ☐

2 🔘 **42** Now listen to the extract. Tick ✓ the topics that are mentioned. Did you guess correctly?

3 What is the main *theme*?

a global warming ☐
b animals and the environment ☐
c recycling ☐
d energy-saving measures ☐

4 Which statement best describes the main *idea*?

a Global warming isn't as serious as people think. ☐
b We can all do something to stop the situation getting worse. ☐
c Earth will never be able to recover from the effects of global warming. ☐
d All life on earth is at risk because of global warming. ☐

5 🔘 **42** Look at the headings below. Listen again to the extract and number each heading in the order you hear the topics (1–5).

Consequences ☐
What governments should do ☐
Statistics ☐1☐
What we can do ☐
Fight for survival ☐

Focus on ...
signposts

Write the correct function (a–c) next to each word or expression.
For instance ☐b☐
Moreover ☐
In addition ☐
For example ☐
To illustrate this ☐
This is why … ☐
Therefore ☐
Also ☐

a to explain consequences
b to give an example
c to list several points

C Listening – Note taking

1 🔊 **42** Listen again to the *Consequences* section of the talk. Compare the notes made by two students.

Jorge's notes

Consequences
1 Ice fields melting (Greenland / Antarctica)
   – sea level (6m?) >> Flooding – millions move
   to higher ground

2 Heat wave – deaths (+ wild fires)
             – crops fail >> millions starve
   · 300,000 a yr soon die

Cynthia's notes

Consequences
Ice in Greenland and Antarctica is melting
faster than anyone had predicted.
Sea levels will rise – up to six metres.
Flooding will affect millions of people living on
coast. Will have to move.
Heat waves more common, people dying from
heat / wild fires (caused by dry conditions).
Severe droughts – crops fail – starvation.
Just a few years / recent study up to
300,000 people a year will die (not counting
impact on animals, birds and fish).

2 **Whose notes do you think are better? Why?**

----

3 🔊 **42** Listen again to the *What we can do* section only. Write notes under each heading.

What we can do

1 Recycling

2 Food

3 Save energy

4 Transport

Did you know …?

Studies show that most students note only 20–40% of the important information of a lecture.

Learning tip

Deciding what is and is not important is a useful listening skill. Look at the audioscript on pages 97–98 and cross out any words that are not important. Then compare with the notes you made in Exercise 3. How accurate were your notes?

Sound smart
Emphasizing important information

1 To emphasize important points, a lecturer might do any one of the following things:
   – slow down
   – pause
   – speak louder
   – say the important words slowly and carefully

2 🔊 **43** Listen to these examples. For each example, decide how the speaker draws attention to the key points. Tick ✓ your answers.

	more slowly	louder	pausing
a		✓	
b			
c			
d			
e			

3 🔊 **44** Listen again to the *What governments should do* section of the talk. Then find the audioscript on page 98 and underline the words and phrases the lecturer emphasizes.

D Speaking – Summarizing a talk

Speaking strategy: Talking about a lecture

1 **When giving an oral summary of a talk, you should:**
   a state the topic
   b review the key points
   c give your opinion

Look at these expressions you can use. Match each expression with a function (a–c).

I think the most interesting part was ☐c☐
Something I didn't agree with was ☐
Basically, it was about ☐
They said / claimed / argued that ☐
There were three main points. ☐

Speak up!

2 **Imagine a friend asks you about the *Humans and the Planet* lecture. Give an oral summary, using your notes to help you.**

Class bonus

Prepare a short one-minute talk giving your view on an environmental issue (global warming, recycling, etc.). Make notes of your ideas. Then practise, emphasizing the important information. Give your talk to the class.

E✗tra practice

Listen to a lecture on the radio in English, or watch a lecture in English on TV. If you wish, note the main ideas and make a list of any signposts you hear the speaker use.

Can-do checklist

Tick what you can do.

	Can do	Need more practice
I can understand the main ideas and themes of a lecture.		
I can take concise notes of detailed, relevant information.		
I can listen for clues such as signposts and style of delivery.		
I can summarize the main points of a talk.		

Get ready to listen and speak

- Match each item of equipment (a–j) with a picture (1–10).
  - a a data projector _6_
  - b a whiteboard ......
  - c an overhead projector ......
  - d a microphone ......
  - e a flipchart ......
  - f marker pens ......
  - g a screen ......
  - h a laser pointer ......
  - i a board rubber ......
  - j overhead transparencies ......

- Look at these factors you need to consider when preparing a presentation. Match each factor with a description.

Objectives	how you want to structure your talk ☐
Audience	how long you have ☐
Content	where you will be giving the talk ☐
Organization	what you want to achieve ☐
Venue	who you are speaking to ☐
Time	what you want to say ☐

- Number each factor in order of importance (1–6).

go to Useful language p. 83

A Listening – Introduction

1 **45** Stephanie Adams is a careers counsellor at a college in the US. She is giving a talk to final year students. Listen and number the stages of her introduction in order (1–4).

introduce the subject ☐
welcome the audience ☐ 1
explain rules for questions ☐
give an overview of the structure of the talk ☐

2 **45** Listen again and complete the expressions Stephanie uses.

a Good ...afternoon, everyone..., and welcome.
b Today I'm .... about job prospects.
c I'll .... describing the current position.
d .... look at salaries.
e ...., I'll move on to career choices.
f And ...., I'll review the main points.
g We'll .... questions at the end.

Did you know ...?

Some experts say the first 30 seconds of your presentation is the most important. How well you start your presentation will affect everything that follows, so it is important to get it right.

B Speaking – Getting off to a good start

1 **Here are some more expressions you can use in your introduction. Write each expression in the correct place.**

The purpose of this presentation is to …
Feel free to interrupt me if you have any questions.
Good morning to you all.
First of all, I'll go over some background details.
Today I want to talk to you about …
After that, I'll move on to …
Then I'll look at …
To start with, I'll review …
Hello. Thank you for giving me this opportunity to …
Finally, I'll review the main points.
I'll start by describing …
I'll make sure we have enough time for questions at the end.

Functions
Welcoming your audience:

Introducing your subject:
The purpose of this presentation is to …

Giving an overview of your talk:

Explaining rules for questions:

Speak up!

2 **Imagine you are giving a talk. Look at the notes below and give your introduction. Use the expressions in Exercise 1 to help you and finish by explaining rules for questions.**

Aim – Business plan for the next five years
1 – where we are now
2 – restructuring plans
3 – expansion into Asia
4 – long-term goals

Example:
You say: Good morning, everyone, and welcome. The purpose of this presentation is to show you our business plan for the next five years. First …

Learning tip

Have you heard of *KISS*? It means **K**eep **I**t **S**hort and **S**imple. In other words, don't use long sentences or difficult grammar. Speak in short, easy-to-understand sentences and avoid using words the audience may not know.

C Listening – Keeping on track

1 **(46) Listen to this extract from the middle of a presentation. Complete the signposts the speaker uses.**

Finishing one point
That's .... about our sales and marketing strategy.

Starting another point
Now I would .... our overseas operations.

Giving an example
To ....example …

2 **(47) Now listen to an extract from a different presentation. Tick ✓ the signposts you hear the speaker use.**

Finishing one point
I've told you about our pensions policy. ☐
We've looked at our pensions policy. ☐

Starting another point
Let me now turn to staff recruitment. ☐
Let's move on to staff recruitment. ☐

Giving an example
A good example of this is … ☐
Another example of this is … ☐

Learning tip

You should maintain good eye contact with your audience throughout your presentation. Make sure you look at all of the audience, not just the people in front of you … and remember to smile!

Sound smart
Sounding confident

1 Most people are nervous when they give a presentation. Here are some tips to remember.

DO
speak slowly
speak calmly

DON'T
speak too quickly
let your voice drop at the end of a sentence

Tips to get attention
Pause between important points.
Lower your voice to draw the audience in.
Raise your voice to emphasize important points.

2 ● 48 Listen to three speakers. Tick ✓ the person you can understand best.
Speaker 1 ☐   Speaker 2 ☐   Speaker 3 ☐

3 ● 48 Listen again and make notes on what was and was not good about each person's performance.
Speaker 1:

Speaker 2:

Speaker 3:

----

4 Look at the audioscript on page 98. Read aloud the words for Speaker 2 and use the tips above to help you sound confident.

D Listening – Concluding your presentation

1 ● 49 Listen to Stephanie Adams conclude her presentation. Number each stage of her conclusion in order (1–3).

thanks the audience ☐
summarizes the main points ☐
invites questions ☐

2 ● 50 Listen and complete these phrases.

Summarizing the main points
a To _____ briefly, then, …
b I'd like to _____ the main points.
c In _____, then …

Thanking your audience
d Thank _____ listening.
e Thank you very _____ attention.

Inviting questions
f Now, does anyone _____ ?
g _____ any questions?
h Are there _____ questions?

3 ● 50 Listen and repeat each phrase.

4 ● 49 Now listen to Stephanie's conclusion again. Tick ✓ the expressions she uses.

E Listening – Questions and answers

● 51 Stephanie has a Q-and-A session at the end of her presentation. How does she encourage questions from the audience? Listen and complete the four phrases.

Sure. Go _____ .
Yes? Please _____ .
Yes, of course. What would you _____ ?
Now, does _____ a question?

F Speaking – Reacting effectively to questions

Speaking strategy: Dealing with questions

1 Notice the expressions you can use when dealing with questions.

I'd like to deal with that question later, if that's all right.

Do you mind if we press on? I'll answer that at the end.

That's a very good point. What does everyone else think?

I'm not quite sure I agree with you on that.

There's no time now, but let's chat about it afterwards.

Speak up!

2 🔊 **52 Imagine you are giving a talk and need to deal with questions. Listen and respond with the most appropriate phrases in Exercise 1.**

Example: a
You hear: Excuse me. Can you explain that last point in more detail?
You say: Do you mind if we press on? I'll answer that at the end.

a   You are worried about time.
b   You think it's a difficult question to answer in a short time.
c   You don't agree.
d   You think it's an interesting question and want to open it up to the audience.
e   You are falling behind and time is short.

G Speaking – Giving a short presentation

Speaking strategy: Keeping it short and simple

1 Prepare to give a short, simple presentation. First, make notes of your ideas.

Decide on a topic. --
List the points you want to make.

Organize the points in the order you want to mention them.

Speak up!

2 Now give your presentation.

Introduction	Welcome the audience.
	Introduce the subject.
	Give an overview of the structure of the talk.
	Explain rules for questions.
Main body	Make your main argument.
	Cover several points.
	Link each one and give examples.
Conclusion	Summarize your argument.
	Thank the audience.

Example: Good morning, everyone. Today I want to talk to you about ...

E X tra practice

Prepare another presentation and this time record yourself. After you finish, listen to your performance and identify any areas you can improve.

Class bonus

Give your presentation to the class, and listen to your classmates' presentations. Use the evaluation form on page 87 to assess each other's performance.

Can-do checklist

Tick what you can do.

	Can do	Need more practice
I can give a short, simple presentation.		
I can structure my talk well and use signposts effectively.		
I can deal with questions from the audience in a variety of ways.		

Unit 16
What do you mean?

Get ready to listen and speak

- Read each statement and tick ✓ your answers.
  In a seminar:
  you are free to express your views. ☐
  you shouldn't ask any questions. ☐
  you should mostly listen and take notes. ☐

  The purpose of a seminar is:
  to encourage open debate. ☐
  to help students learn from each other. ☐
  to explore a topic in more detail. ☐

- Write *T* (True) or *F* (False) for each statement.
  You don't need to prepare for a seminar. ......
  You shouldn't interrupt anyone. ......
  The success of the seminar depends on the teacher. ......

go to Useful language p. 83

A Listening – Starting your seminar

1 🔘 **53** Look at the advice in the *Study skills* sheet.
Then listen to Greg start his talk in a seminar. How
well does he cover the points (1–4)?

----

2 **What is the topic of Greg's talk?**

Study skills –
Advice for students

Starting your seminar

1 Say what the topic is.

2 Say why you have chosen that
  topic.

3 Outline the structure of the talk.

4 Give a summary of the theory.

3 🔘 **53** Listen again and complete the form.

Learning style	Advice for studying
V	....
A	....
R	....
K	....

4 What's your view of Greg's talk so far? Tick ✓ your answers.

		Yes	No
a	Are the aims clear?	☐	☐
b	Has the talk been well prepared?	☐	☐
c	Is it well organized?	☐	☐
d	Is there any waste, i.e. repetition?	☐	☐
e	Is the argument easy to follow?	☐	☐
f	Does the speaker sound confident?	☐	☐

5 a What is your general impression of this part of Greg's talk?

very good ☐   good ☐   OK ☐   poor ☐

Learning tip

When giving a talk in a seminar, don't just read aloud from a prepared script. Refer to notes, and try to speak to the audience and engage them directly.

Did you know ...?

The more enthusiastic you appear and sound, the more interested your audience will be in what you have to say. Remember that your body language can help you get across your point effectively. Use gestures to help explain what you mean, and don't forget to engage with your audience by maintaining good eye contact.

B Listening – Presenting an argument

1 ● 54 Read the statements below. Then listen to the last part of Greg's talk and tick ✓ your answers.

Greg thinks:	Yes	No
a most people have the same learning style.	☐	✓
b one learning style is better than the rest.	☐	☐
c people learn in similar ways.	☐	☐
d it's not possible to categorize everyone.	☐	☐
e the human brain is predictable.	☐	☐

2 Tick ✓ which statement most closely matches Greg's personal opinion.

a We all have more than one learning style, but we usually rely on one or two most of the time. ☐

b By categorizing learning styles, we can help people to learn very effectively. ☐

c It is not possible to analyze learning styles because we learn in too many different ways. ☐

d More research into how people learn is necessary. ☐

Sound smart
Sounding enthusiastic

1 You can sound enthusiastic when you speak by:
   - raising the pitch of your voice
   - emphasizing the key words
   - making your voice go up and down more than usual

2 ● 55 Listen to the same extract, spoken in two different ways. Tick ✓ which sounds more enthusiastic.
   Speaker 1 ☐   Speaker 2 ☐

3 ● 55 Now find the audioscript on page 99. Then listen again to the more enthusiastic speaker and read aloud the speaker's words at the same time.

Study skills – Advice for students

After you have covered the theory behind your topic, you should give your personal opinion and comments. Present an argument to explain your views and justify them.

C Speaking – Making a good case

Speaking strategy: Reinforcing your argument

1 **To make your point more forcefully, repeat it in a different way. Here are some expressions you can use.**

In other words, …
To put it another way, …
The point I'm making is …
What I'm getting at is …

2 (154) **Listen again to Greg present his conclusion. Tick ✓ the expressions he uses.**

Learning tip

Be aware of your body language while you are giving a talk. Avoid distracting movements, such as playing with a pen or walking forwards and backwards.

Speak up!

3 **Imagine you are making an argument and want to reinforce your point. Rephrase each of these statements, using the expressions in Exercise 1.**

Example: a Knowing what learning style you are doesn't make any difference to your ability to learn.
You say: What I'm getting at is there is no benefit to analyzing learning styles.

a Knowing what learning style you are doesn't make any difference to your ability to learn.
b Information we receive isn't always 'learned' in the way we may think.
c There is almost no evidence to suggest that one model of learning style is more accurate than another.

D Listening – Debating issues

1 **Greg has finished his talk and asks for questions. Before you listen, note some questions you would like to ask about learning styles.**

2 (156) **Listen to the final discussion stage of Greg's talk. Does anyone ask one of your questions?**

3 (156) **Look at the chart on the right. Then listen once more and note Greg's answers to each question.**

4 **How well do you think Greg answers each question?**

Questions	Answers
Advantages of being mulitmodal?	
Is VARK a learning style?	
Are learning styles fixed?	
Men–women differences?	

E Speaking – In a discussion

Speaking strategy: Following up a question

1 If you feel your question has not been answered, you can rephrase the question and ask it again. Here are some expressions you can use.

That's not really what I was asking. I meant …

Sorry. I'm still not very clear about …

I think you've answered a slightly different question. What I want to know is …

Perhaps my question wasn't very clear. Actually, I was asking …

2 🔊56 Listen again to the extract. Which of the expressions above do you hear?

Speak up!

3 Imagine you have asked a question, but feel that it hasn't been answered fully. Use the expressions in Exercise 1 to rephrase each question (a–c).

Example: a

You say: Sorry. I'm still not very clear about how we can find our own learning style.

a How do we find our own learning style?
b What's the value of studying learning styles?
c If we study all the learning styles, will we become better learners?

Did you know …?

In the VARK test, men have more kinaesthetic responses and women have more read / write responses.

Class bonus

1 Prepare a short talk on a topic of your choice. Then give your talk to the class.
2 Listen to your classmates' presentations. Grade each one, using Appendix 4 on page 87.

E ✗tra practice

Go to the VARK test website and try the VARK questionnaire for yourself. Answer the questions and then check your result. Tell a friend about the type of learner you are.

You can take the VARK test at http://www.vark-learn.com/

Can-do checklist

Tick what you can do.

	Can do	Need more practice
I can understand the basic principles of giving a seminar.		
I can present a well-organized argument and reinforce key points.		
I can follow up a question if I feel it hasn't been answered fully.		
I can evaluate my own performance.		

Section 1

🔵 **57** **Listen and reply to each statement you hear. Circle your answer.**

Example:
You hear: What time would be most convenient for you?
a That would be fine.
ⓑ Between four and five.
c Yes, it is.

1
a Is that your best offer?
b I think you're absolutely right.
c I don't see it like that at all.

2
a Yes, I got it all.
b Yes, I'll get it.
c I had it.

3
a Is that your final answer?
b I have no problem with that.
c You're welcome.

4
a I'm afraid so.
b Yes, I have a question.
c Yes, let's move on.

5
a What do you mean by that?
b I definitely agree.
c Yes, that's right.

6
a Yes, that would be fine.
b Is that your best offer?
c Perhaps you can give me your opinion?

7
a I'm afraid not.
b Is tomorrow morning OK?
c Yes, that's fine.

8
a That's not a problem.
b Yes, he did.
c No, the line was engaged.

9
a Yes, it is.
b It's Gabrielle from Sales.
c That's right.

10
a What's your opinion?
b It's a deal.
c Thanks.

Section 2

🔵 **58** **Read each situation. Then listen and write the letter.**

Example:
You want to ask the delivery company to deliver the package before 5 pm today. What do you say?
You hear:
a Do you think you can deliver before 5 pm today?
b When would be a good time to deliver?
c It won't be until late afternoon, I'm afraid.
You write: a

1 The photocopier in your office is broken, but the repair company can't come for three days. What do you say?
....

2 You haven't understood what someone said to you. What do you say? ....

3 You call a colleague, but they are not available. You want to leave a message for them. What do you say? ....

4 Someone has misunderstood what you said. What do you say? ....

5 A colleague just told you they are quitting the company. You want to check you heard correctly. What do you say?
....

6 You want to arrange a meeting with a colleague at three. What do you say? ....

7 A customer asks to speak to a colleague, but your colleague isn't there. What do you say? ....

8 You didn't understand what someone said, so you want them to repeat it for you. What do you say? ....

9 You are giving a talk when someone raises their hand to ask a question. What do you say? ....

10 You want to start your presentation. What do you say?
....

Section 3

Read each situation and (circle) your answer.

Example:
Which is the best phrase to use when trying to bargain with someone?
a Do you think you could … ?
b I really must insist that …
(c) If you …, then I'll …

1 Your surname is Branson, but the person you are speaking to said Manson. Do you …
   a say nothing as it's not important?
   b repeat your surname with emphasis to correct the mistake?
   c write your surname down on some paper and give it to the person?

2 If someone asks you to take a message, should you …
   a write the message in full?
   b write only the main points and summarize to confirm?
   c ask the caller to send an email just to be safe?

3 Which of these phrases can you use to disagree with an idea?
   a I have no problem with that.
   b I don't think you understand what I mean.
   c I'm afraid I'm not very keen on that.

4 What phrase should you use if someone says a word you don't know?
   a So that means …
   b Sorry. You can't expect me to understand that.
   c Can you explain what … means, please?

5 Before you make an important call, it's sometimes a good idea to …
   a write down everything you want to say.
   b make a brief note of what you want to say.
   c practise the conversation with a colleague.

6 When you are listening and taking notes, you should …
   a note down everything you can.
   b only note the key words.
   c close your eyes sometimes to help you concentrate.

7 Why is it a good idea to identify the information you need before you listen?
   a It helps you focus your listening on only the details you need.
   b You will have more time to listen for other details.
   c You can answer the questions faster that way.

8 When giving a lecture in English, how can you emphasize important points?
   a By speaking quickly, so you can repeat the point many times.
   b By pausing between important points.
   c By coughing to get the audience's attention.

9 What's a good way to make sure you have understood what someone said?
   a Write it down and check later.
   b Look carefully at them to see how they are feeling.
   c Repeat what they said, beginning with *So you're saying that …?*

10 You are giving a talk when someone raises their hand to ask a question. What can you not say?
   a That's a very good point. What does everyone else think?
   b There'll be time for questions at the end.
   c I'd like to deal with questions later, if that's all right.

Section 4

Read each statement and write your reply.

Example:
I'd like three black filing cabinets and a pack of A3 envelopes, please.
Certainly. Do you want to order anything else?

1 Do you mind if we press on?
----

2 I'm sorry. We can't fix the photocopier until Friday next week.
----

3 So what did the thief look like?
----

4 You mustn't keep putting the cart before the horse.
----

5 If you sign the contract today, I'll give you a ten percent discount.
----

6 Can you give me an overview of your talk, please?
----

7 What time would be most suitable for you?
----

8 So you think we need to expand faster into Europe and Asia?
----

9 Can you describe the bag that you lost?
----

10 Please leave a message after the tone.

Appendix 1
Useful language

This appendix contains a list of expressions which are useful when carrying out the listening and speaking tasks in each unit. The expressions are divided into *Things you can say* and *Things you might hear*.

You can use this appendix in the following ways.

Before you begin each unit, do one of the following:
1 Look at the expressions and use your dictionary to check the meaning of any words you do not understand.
2 Look at the expressions, but try to work out the meaning of any words you do not understand *when you see or hear them in the unit*. This is more challenging, but it is a very useful skill to practise.

After you complete each unit:
3 Look at the expressions and check that you understand them. Try to think of different examples using the same key words. Find the key words and expressions in the *Audioscript* to see them in context.
4 Listen to the expressions, and notice the stress and rhythm of the speaker. You may want to mark sentence stress in a highlighter pen. Listen again and repeat each expression, practising the stress and rhythm.
5 Listen again to the expressions and notice the pronunciation of any difficult words. You may want to mark word stress in a highlighter pen. Listen once more and repeat each word, practising the word stress.
6 Cover a column. Then listen to each expression and repeat from memory. This helps to focus your listening.

Unit 1

Things you can say	Things you might hear
Hi there.	Long time no see.
How's it going?	See you around.
How are you doing?	I think so too.
What's up?	Definitely.
I've got to go.	That's not right!
Right, I must dash.	No way!
I guess I'd better be going.	I don't agree.
It was nice talking with you.	I don't think so.
See you later.	From my point of view, …
Talk to you later.	It seems to me that …
Have a nice weekend.	In my opinion, …
See you around.	If you ask me, …
Right. I'm off!	
It was lovely to see you.	
I should get going (I suppose).	
It's been great to talk with you.	
I know what you mean, but …	
I may be wrong, but …	
I agree to some extent, but …	

Unit2

Things you can say	Things you might hear
I've booked a table for eight o'clock. Can we have a little more time? For starter I'd like … Oh, it looks lovely! Thank you. I'll have an orange juice. Can I have the bill, please? No, I'll pay. Really, I insist. Sorry, but I've been waiting for my main course for twenty minutes. Excuse me. I'm afraid I don't like this wine. I think it might be corked. I think this bill is wrong. I've been charged too much.	Follow me, please. Are you ready to order? And for main course? Would you like anything to drink? Would you like dessert? This is our house special. No, you paid last time. Let me get it. I'll get you another one right away. I'll find out what's happened to it. I forgot to mention it.

Unit3

Things you can say	Things you might hear
I'm looking for a flat, with two bedrooms. We'd like a place with a garage. Would you mind if I painted the lounge white? Is it OK if I buy a new sofa? I was wondering if I could have broadband Internet installed? Could you send someone to repair the washing machine, please? I'm not very happy about this at all. I'd like to know what you are going to do about it.	They all come furnished. The rent is $795 per month. It is due on the first of each month (one month in advance). The deposit is six weeks' rent. This is refundable at the end of your tenancy. Electricity, gas and telephone bills have to be set up independently. You will have to pay a cancellation fee. We will send someone to repair it at no charge. If you break the terms of your tenancy agreement, you can be evicted. I'll get someone to fix it today.

Unit4

Things you can say	Things you might hear
I bought this notebook computer yesterday, but I'm afraid that the monitor doesn't work. Sorry, but the radio I bought last week has stopped working. I see. You'll either repair it or replace it. What about a refund? So, all faults and accidental damage are covered? It's a bit more than I wanted to pay. Is that your best price? Can't you do any better? How much for cash? Well, I'll give you £20 for it. OK, that's fine. It's a deal. That's OK with me.	Do you have a receipt? You can't use a credit voucher to buy anything that's in the sale. We don't give refunds, I'm afraid. It isn't under guarantee, so we can't really help you. This sofa comes with a full two-year guarantee, covering faults, and accidental damage. You'll only have a refund if a replacement isn't available. That's £35 to you. Let's say £30, then. How's that? It's a bargain, I promise you. That is a cash price! It's a deal.

Unit 5

Things you can say	Things you might hear
I think the characters are so funny. The animation is great, too. It's a classic. I can't stand soap operas. I don't think I've missed a single episode. I didn't use to like it when it first started, but now I'm really into it. I'm not very keen on it, really. The acting is totally convincing. The plot is so ridiculous that I can't watch it.	Thanks to the sensitive direction, the whole film blends together well. Without doubt, it's the must-see movie of the year. The warning signs have been here for ages. We haven't done anything about it. As a result, animals like polar bears will become extinct. As sea levels rise, more and more land will be lost to the sea. Hundreds of thousands of people will have to move home. It's OK for people alive today, but it will be a big, big problem for our children and the generations to come.

Unit 6

Things you can say	Things you might hear
I think I'm coming down with the flu. It started last week. I've been feeling like this since yesterday. I've got a runny nose, a sore throat and a headache, as well. I feel a little feverish. I've been taking some aspirin. Oh, I'm sorry to hear that. Well, that's good news. How awful! Oh, no! That's terrible. Thank goodness for that! Oh, dear. Really? What a relief!	What seems to be the trouble? Do you know when it started? How long have you been feeling like this? Where does it hurt exactly? Is it painful if I do this? Do you know if you are allergic to anything? Have you got any other symptoms? Have you been taking anything for it? Well, I'd better take a look. I recommend aspirin to relieve the aches and pains. You should drink lots of water and stay in bed. The problem should go in a couple of days. You need to exercise more often.

Unit 7

Things you can say	Things you might hear
OK. That's good to know. Thanks for the tip. That sounds worth a visit. What time does it leave? Where exactly does it leave from? How long does it last? What exactly is included? Is there anything you have to pay extra for? What range of cars do you have? Is insurance included? Do I have to pay an excess if I have an accident? Can I hire a car one-way? Is there a mileage limit? Do you provide child car seats? Is accident cover included? What documents do I need?	I recommend staying there. You should definitely hire a car. I recommend you stay at the Emerald Lake Lodge. It's a perfect place to explore from. It's expensive, but it's well worth going there. It's not really worth staying there too long. We'll pick you up by bus outside the hotel. Full cover is provided for every named driver. There's a 24-hour emergency number to call if you need assistance. You need a valid driver's licence or an international licence with a passport. What class of car would you like to have? Actually, we have a special offer on at the moment.

Unit 8

Things you can say	Things you might hear
I was wondering if you could suggest a good place to stay?	Have you found anywhere to stay?
I wonder if you would mind giving me a bit of advice about	It should be quite reasonable.
the weather?	It's really lively because it's the student area.
Do you think you could tell me how best to get around the	The Metro is usually quite crowded, but you can get anywhere
city?	you want and it doesn't cost much.
I don't suppose you know anywhere good to eat?	When I go, I usually just use my bank card and get cash from
Do you think I should exchange money at a bank or bureau de	ATMs.
change?	It's as safe as any other city, I think.
Is it worth visiting the aquarium?	This is where the Spanish founded the city, in 1535.
Do you think it's a good idea to walk to the castle, or is it too	You can see the Government Palace, where the President
far?	lives.
Would you recommend going to the National Museum?	Over there is the cathedral to the east.
Excuse me. I have a question.	This is the exact spot where the old castle used to be.
Could I interrupt for a moment?	Of course. Go ahead.
Could you tell us a bit more about them?	I'd rather you let me finish, if that's all right.

Unit 9

Things you can say	Things you might hear
We've got a problem with our photocopier.	I'll have a look and see what we can do.
The paper's jammed and we can't fix it.	It looks like we might be able to get someone to you this
Don't you have anything a bit earlier?	morning.
I'm sorry, but that's no good at all.	When would be a good time for someone to call?
Sorry, but you have to do something sooner.	I'm sorry. We won't be able to repair it for at least four weeks.
It's simply not acceptable to leave it that long.	I'm afraid we can't send anyone until tomorrow afternoon.
I really must insist that you do something about this right away.	If you order now, we'll give you an eight percent reduction.
Is that your best offer?	If you pay in advance, we'll promise free delivery.
	We might be able to offer free installation if you order two.
	I'll give one-year free insurance, provided that you order in bulk.

Unit 10

Things you can say	Things you might hear
I'd like to open an account, please.	I'll need to see some form of identification, such as your
I'd like to pay this cheque into my current account, please.	passport, or driving licence.
Can I send some money abroad from here?	I can certainly order a replacement for you here.
I want to deposit this money into my savings account.	You need to telephone our 24-hour emergency number to
I'd like to buy some traveller's cheques, please.	report it.
Could I see someone to arrange an overdraft, please?	Can I have your paying-in slip and your bank card, too, please?
Does that mean I can get at the money immediately?	Utility bills take seven working days to go through.
So that means if I save over £25,000, I'll get 3.5% interest?	Which type of savings account do you want?
Do you mean that I can't withdraw the money for three years?	If you want to withdraw some money, then you should give
So you're saying that I have to pay £295 if I want this account?	30 days' notice.
What do you mean by 'penalty'?	If you take money out, you won't get any interest for that
I'm sorry. Can you explain what 'variable' means?	month.
Could you say that again?	You have to apply online for that.
I'm sorry, but I didn't quite catch that.	We can't do it here in the branch.
I don't quite get what you mean.	
Can you run that by me again, please?	

Unit 11

Things you can say	Things you might hear
He's short and stocky with long, wavy dark hair and a square face. He looks in his early 20s and he's quite scruffy. He's slightly overweight. He's wearing a blue jacket and a patterned tie. She's medium height, rather skinny and she looks in her 30s. She looks very smart. She's got some black high heels on and she's carrying a briefcase. He's got on a pair of white running shoes. She looks fairly casual. It's a small, black leather bag, with a zip along the top and a shoulder strap.	Just let me get the right form. Can you describe the bag? Are there any distinguishing marks on it? Which service do you require? Where do you need the ambulance to come to? What has happened there? How many people are hurt? What exactly did you see? How fast was the car travelling? So how did the car hit the cyclist? Was the cyclist on the wrong side of the road? What about the car? So the collision happened here, you say?

Unit 12

Things you can say	Things you might hear
Can you put me through? When shall I give you a ring? I always get the engaged signal. Right. I think I've got that. Let me repeat that, just to make sure. I'll just go over that to confirm. Sorry. What was that last part again, please? Could I leave a message, please? Does that make sense? Do you think you could take a message? Would you mind taking a message? I appreciate your help. Thank you.	I'm afraid he's out of the office right now. Would you like to leave a message? I'll make sure he gets that. Does he know what number to contact you on? Please don't hang up. I'll just put you on hold. Can I call you back later? It's great to hear from you. Can I ask who's calling? Have you got that? Who is this, please? Sorry. I didn't get your name. Could you repeat that back?

Unit 13

Things you can say	Things you might hear
I think you're absolutely right. That's not right at all. I think we're drifting off the point a bit. Right, now let's move on, shall we? Can you explain what you mean by that? Could I come in here, please? Let's get down to business, shall we? That sounds reasonable to me. I have no problem with that. I'm afraid that's not how I see it. I'm not very keen on that idea at all. That's not quite what I meant. Sorry. I think you've misunderstood me. I'm afraid you haven't understood what I'm getting at.	Let's take a vote. Mrs Kendry is chair for this meeting. What's on the agenda? Who's going to take the minutes? What are the objectives of this meeting? It was decided by a show of hands. I'd like to start by asking … Do you have any thoughts? Perhaps you can give us your opinion? How do you feel about that? I'll quickly go over today's main points. I think we've covered everything, so shall we call it a day? It looks like we can finish early today. We'll have to cut this meeting short, I'm afraid.

Unit 14

Things you can say	Things you might hear
A good lecture should be informative. The main theme is global warming. These notes are better because … The lecturer emphasized important points.	Here at the Engineering Department we pride ourselves on our health and safety record. We have recently updated and improved all our resources and equipment. One main area of interest here, both theoretical and in its practical applications, is the area of sustainable energy technologies. The figures are staggering. So, what can we do?

Unit 15

Things you can say	Things you might hear
Good morning to you all. Thank you for giving me this opportunity to … The purpose of this presentation is to … Today I want to talk to you about … First of all, I'll go over some background details. To start with, I'll review … I'll start by describing … Then I'll look at … After that, I'll move on to … Finally, I'll review the main points. Feel free to interrupt me if you have any questions. I'll make sure we have enough time for questions at the end.	Do you mind if we press on? I'll answer that at the end. There's no time now, but let's chat about it afterwards. Can I answer any questions? Are there any final questions? I'll try to answer any questions you may have. Sure. Go ahead Yes? Please ask your question. Yes, of course. What would you like to know? Now, does anyone else have a question? I'm not quite sure I agree with you on that. That's a very good point. What does everyone else think?

Unit 16

Things you can say	Things you might hear
What I'm getting at is … The point I'm making is that … In other words, … That's not really what I was asking. I meant … I think you've answered a slightly different question. What I want to know is … Sorry. I'm still not very clear about … Perhaps my question wasn't very clear. Actually, I was asking you to say …	I'll start by outlining four competing theories about how people learn. So, that's basically what I want to say about this for now. Are there any questions?

Appendix 2
Pronunciation features

Sound smart gives additional guidance to help you develop your pronunciation skills. You will find at least one **Sound smart** in each unit of this book.
This appendix contains a list of the pronunciation areas covered in **Sound smart** at this level.

You can use this appendix in the following ways:

1 Choose a pronunciation focus you want to practise. Go to the unit where the **Sound smart** section appears and practise again.
2 Find a pronunciation focus that you think is especially useful. Practise once more, but this time record yourself and listen afterwards. Try to identify areas you can improve.
3 Practise again, but this time listen to a different recording. Look in the audioscript first to find a suitable recording.

Practise each pronunciation focus in **Sound smart** several times. The more you practise, the better your pronunciation will become.

List of pronunciation areas covered in *Sound smart*

Unit 1	Intonation in question tags
Unit 2	The schwa /ə/
Unit 3	–
Unit 4	Showing emotion
Unit 5	Stress and rhythm
Unit 6	Linking /w/ and /j/
Unit 7	Missing sounds /t/, /d/ and /h/
Unit 8	Linking consonant–vowel
Unit 9	Using stress for emphasis
Unit 10	Corrective stress
Unit 11	The schwa /ə/
Unit 12	–
Unit 13	Intonation in questions
Unit 14	Emphasizing important information
Unit 15	Sounding confident
Unit 16	–

Appendix 3
Speaking strategies

Speaking strategies are useful techniques to help you communicate in a wide variety of situations. You will find several **Speaking strategies** in most units of this book. This appendix contains a list of the **Speaking strategies** covered at this level.

You can use this appendix in the following ways:

1 Choose a strategy you want to practise. Go to the unit where the strategy appears and practise again.
2 Find a strategy that you think is especially useful. Practise once more, but this time record yourself and listen afterwards. Try to identify areas you can improve. If possible, practise with an English-speaking friend.

Practise each strategy several times. The more you practise, the easier it will be to use the strategies when you need them in real life.

List of *Speaking strategies* covered

Unit 1	Agreeing Asking follow-up questions Arguing your point
Unit 2	Offering to pay Complaining in a restaurant
Unit 3	Asking about alternatives Making requests and asking for permission Making your point more forcefully
Unit 4	Making a complaint in a shop Checking important points Reaching an agreement
Unit 5	Talking about films Summarizing
Unit 6	Describing symptoms Showing concern and relief
Unit 7	Making recommendations Responding to recommendations Asking for detailed information
Unit 8	Making polite requests Asking for recommendations Interrupting politely Asking for further details
Unit 9	Fixing a time Insisting Bargaining
Unit 10	Making sure you understand Asking for clarification Asking someone to repeat

Unit 11	Describing someone's appearance Describing things Getting to the point
Unit 12	Repeating key information Asking for clarification Leaving effective messages
Unit 13	Bringing someone into a discussion Accepting and rejecting suggestions Correcting misunderstandings
Unit 14	Talking about a lecture
Unit 15	Starting your presentation Dealing with questions Keeping it short and simple
Unit 16	Reinforcing your argument Following up a question

Appendix 4
Presentation evaluation

This appendix contains an evaluation form for assessing presentations, and a separate form for recording feedback on your own performance. You can use this appendix in the following ways:

In class

Listening to a presentation:
While you listen to a classmate give a presentation, consider each question on the **Presentation evaluation** form and give a grade. Give a final grade for your overall impression, and note any areas you think are especially good, or that need attention. Then tell your classmate your opinion, and add some suggestions to help them improve.

Giving a presentation:
After you have given a presentation, listen to your classmates' opinions of your performance and make a note of their grades on the *My performance* form. Note any strengths and weaknesses, and listen carefully to any suggestions for improvement. Study the feedback and try to improve on any areas of weakness.

For self-study

Listen to a talk or presentation on the radio, or television. Consider each question on the **Presentation evaluation** form and give the speaker a grade. Note any areas you think are especially good, or weak, and give a final grade for your overall impression. Ask yourself how the speaker could improve.

Presentation evaluation

		Excellent		Satisfactory		Weak	

Organization

	Excellent		Satisfactory		Weak	
Were the aims clear?	6	5	4	3	2	1
Were the ideas clearly linked?	6	5	4	3	2	1
Was the summary effective?	6	5	4	3	2	1

Content

Were the facts and information accurate?	6	5	4	3	2	1
Was the content relevant to the topic?	6	5	4	3	2	1
Did the talk hold the audience's attention?	6	5	4	3	2	1
Did the speaker deal with questions effectively?	6	5	4	3	2	1

Language

Was the speaker's language accurate?	6	5	4	3	2	1
Did the speaker use a wide range of vocabulary?	6	5	4	3	2	1
Did the speaker use signposts effectively?	6	5	4	3	2	1

Delivery

Was the speaker's voice clear and easy to understand?	6	5	4	3	2	1
Was the speed and volume appropriate?	6	5	4	3	2	1
Did the speaker emphasize important points well?	6	5	4	3	2	1

Body language

Did the speaker use gestures where appropriate?	6	5	4	3	2	1
Did the speaker maintain good eye contact?	6	5	4	3	2	1
Did the speaker appear relaxed and in control?	6	5	4	3	2	1

Visual aids

Were any visual aids clear and well presented?	6	5	4	3	2	1
Did the speaker exploit the visual aids fully?	6	5	4	3	2	1

What is your overall impression of the talk? 6 5 4 3 2 1

Good points: _____

Weak points: _____

Suggestions for improvement: _____

My performance

	Group's grades	Group's comments
Organization		
Content		
Language		
Delivery		
Body language		
Visual aids		
Overall impression		

My strengths: _____

My weaknesses: _____

Group's suggestions for improvement: _____

Audioscript

These recordings are mostly in standard British English accents. Where a speaker has a different accent, it is noted in brackets.

 CD1 Social and Travel

Unit 1

 2

1
Jane: Morning, Mike.
Mike: Oh, hi there, Jane. What's up?
Jane: Nothing much. I'm just taking these back to the library. How about you?
Mike: Oh, you know. Same old thing.

2 (Sukrishna = Indian; Raúl = Spanish)
Raúl: Right, I'm off! Thanks for inviting me, Sukrishna. That was great.
Sukrishna: Glad you could come, Raúl. It was lovely to see you.
Raúl: You too. Well, take care. Bye!

3 (Ian and Sue = American)
Ian: Hey, Sue! Long time no see.
Sue: Ian? How are you doing?
Ian: Pretty good, thanks. And you?
Sue: Oh, I'm doing OK. I just went to the mall.*
Ian: Me too!

4 (Miki = Japanese; Kevin = Canadian)
Kevin: Well, I should get going, I suppose. I have to get back to work.
Miki: OK, then. It's been great to talk with you.
Kevin: Maybe we can do this again sometime, Miki?
Miki: Sure, Kevin. I'd like that.

↻**Did you notice?**
In American English, people often say *I just went* … In British English, this would be a mistake. A native British English speaker would say *I've just been* …

3 (Martin = Australian; Ana = Brazilian)
Martin: Hi there. How's it going?
Ana: Good, thanks.
Martin: I'm Martin. Are you new here? I haven't seen you around.
Ana: Yes. I only started on Monday.
Martin: Great. So, what department are you in?
Ana: Housekeeping.
Martin: Oh, yeah? I work on reception.
Ana: I see. Are you American?
Martin: No, I'm from Sydney, Australia. How about you?
Ana: I'm from Brazil. How long have you been here in Singapore?
Martin: Nearly three years now. I like it a lot.
Ana: Me too. I love it.
Martin: So, how are you enjoying the job so far?
Ana: It's great. Everyone's been really friendly.

Martin: Where were you before you moved here?
Ana: At the Regent Palace, in London.
Martin: That's a big place, isn't it?
Ana: Yes, it has around 900 bedrooms. London's a city too big for me*. I don't like big cities.
Martin: Me neither. Anyway, I've got to go. It was nice talking with you.
Ana: You too. See you around.

↻**Did you notice?**
Ana says *London's a city too big for me.* A native speaker would probably say *London's too big for me.*

4 (d–f = American; g–j = Chinese)
a   I don't like chicken.
b   I'm going to the party tomorrow.
c   I like watching old black and white films.
d   I can't drive.
e   I won't go shopping this afternoon.
f   I've been to Rome twice.
g   I didn't sleep well last night.
h   I've never been to a live concert.
i   I'm not feeling very well.
j   I did some gardening at the weekend.

5
a   I read a book at the weekend, but it was terrible.
b   My sister's just had a baby.
c   I used to do a lot of sport, you know, when I was younger.
d   I haven't seen my parents for a long time.
e   I'm going to go to the city centre this afternoon.

6
A   Helen lives in Hong Kong, doesn't she?
B   Helen lives in Hong Kong, doesn't she?

7
a   Sam and Kevin are divorced, aren't they?
b   You don't want to go out tonight, do you?
c   Jason can speak French, can't he?
d   You haven't eaten dinner yet, have you?
e   She won't come to the party, will she?
f   I didn't forget your birthday, did I?
g   He looks much younger than her, doesn't he?
h   We're not going in there, are we?
i   Everything will be all right, won't it?
j   I'm not late, am I?

8 (1A = Chinese; 4 = Japanese;
5 = South African; 6 = American)
1   A: I think there are too many of them. Kids are under too much pressure at school.
    B: That's exactly what I think. There should be more learning rather than testing.

2   A: From my point of view, if you don't eat meat, you can't have a balanced diet.
    B: That's not right at all! You don't have to eat meat to be healthy.
3   A: It seems to me that there should be a limit on the number of cars and lorries. The situation is getting out of control.
    B: I couldn't agree more. The government should definitely do something.
4   A: I believe that if you fancy a cigarette in a restaurant after a nice meal, then you should be able to have one.
    B: No way! I don't agree. The smell is terrible.
5   A: I feel it's going to be a huge health problem in a few years' time.
    B: I think so too. Definitely. It's bad for the body to be overweight, but people just don't seem to listen.
6   A: Well, I think they are bad for kids. I mean, they spend all day staring at the screen, rather than playing with friends.
    B: I don't think so. They can learn a lot by playing these things too, you know.

9 (a = French; b = German; c = Egyptian;
e = Canadian)
a   I think politicians these days are all the same.
b   I believe that marriage should be for life.
c   From my point of view, killing animals for sport is wrong.
d   It seems to me that the world is getting more dangerous.
e   In my opinion, working overtime is too stressful.

10 (a = French; b = German; c = Egyptian;
d = Italian; e = Canadian)
a   If you ask me, there are too many cars on the roads these days.
b   I think mothers shouldn't work if they have young children.
c   In my opinion, studying for a degree is getting too expensive.
d   I think taxes should be lower.
e   It seems to me that we rely on computers too much these days.

Unit 2

11 (Waiter = Canadian)
a   Can I take your coat?
b   Is everything OK with your meal?
c   Are you ready to order?
d   Would you like anything to drink first?
e   Here's your main course … the steak.
f   Have you made a reservation?
g   Would you like some more wine?
h   Can I get you any dessert?

💿12 (Customer = Japanese; Waiter = Canadian)
1 Customer: Hello. I booked a table for seven o'clock. The name's Katai.
  Waiter: Ah, yes. Follow me, please.
2 Waiter: Are you ready to order?
  Customer: Yes, for starter I'd like the soup, please.
  Waiter: And for your main course?
  Customer: I'll have the salmon, thank you.
  Waiter: Very good. And would you like anything to drink?
  Customer: Just some mineral water, please.
3 Waiter: Would you like dessert?
  Customer: No, thanks. I'm full. Can I have the bill, please?

💿13 (Waitress = Italian)
Ah, yes, this is a lovely starter. It's toasted bread with tomatoes, garlic on top, some basil, olive oil, little cheese*. Very tasty. So, one bruschetta?
This is our house special. Fresh pasta with cheese inside, a tomato and cream sauce. Quite sweet, but if you like ravioli, you'll love it.
Which? This? The second one? This is fried chicken with sautéed potatoes, tomatoes, mushroom and roast red peppers. I'm from Toscana, so I like this one! A little salty, but very good.
Yes, this is grilled beef. Very tender, with a special gravy made from Barolo wine and mushrooms … Bistecca is always very popular with the English.
This is a kind of sponge cake. Very light, with lots of cream, and chocolate on top, but it has coffee, a little wine and sugar inside, so it gives you energy. I think 'Tiramisù' means 'Pick me up' in English.

↪ ***Did you notice?***
The waitress says *little cheese*. A native speaker would say *a little cheese*.

💿14
tender medium under-done wonderful
salmon sugar

💿15
waiter reservation potato pasta starter
popular

💿16 (Speaker = American)
Oh, look. Here's the bill. I'll get it.
Well, shall we at least split it?
Are you sure?
Thanks very much.

💿17 (A = customer; B = waitress)
a A: We've been waiting for our drinks for half an hour.
  B: Sorry, I'll bring them for you now.
b A: Excuse me. These carrots are almost raw.
  B: Oh, dear. I'll get some more for you.
c A: I'm afraid I asked for it rare, but this steak is virtually well-done.

B: Sorry, sir. I'll bring you another one as quickly as possible.
d A: I didn't know this dish had nuts in it. I'm allergic to them.
  B: Sorry, sir. I forgot to mention it. Would you like to order a different main course?
e A: Don't you have any high chairs for children to sit in?
  B: I'm afraid not. Would a cushion do?
f A: Sorry, but I asked for the bill ten minutes ago.
  B: I'll find out what's happened to it.

💿18
Well, I went to two very different restaurants this week. The first was The Big Bistro, on King's Street. As its name suggests, it was big, although the atmosphere was quite sophisticated. The staff were professional and the service was very attentive. The food, though, was disappointing. My tuna salad starter was unimaginative and the steak I had for the main course was rather tough. The potatoes were undercooked, too. The meal cost £17, but with £5 for a glass of wine and £3 tip on top, I'd say it was not good value for money, so just six out of ten … The second restaurant was Sala Thai on Gilbert Road. An independent restaurant rather than a big chain, the atmosphere here was relaxed and inviting, and the staff were all very friendly. The service was excellent. I had a hot and spicy soup to start with, which was very enjoyable, and for the main course a very tasty fish dish. Absolutely delicious. It was cheap, too – just £20 including drinks and service, so I'd say Sala Thai is definitely worth a visit. Nine out of ten.

Unit3

💿19 (Agent = Irish; Oleg = Russian)
Agent: Carter Property Management. Can I help you?
Oleg: Oh, hello. Erm. Yes. I'm looking for a place near Trinity College.
Agent: I see. Can I take your name, please?
Oleg: Yes, it's Oleg Markov.
Agent: How do you spell that?
Oleg: O-L-E-G, Markov, M-A-R-K-O-V. Yes. I'm looking for a flat, with two bedrooms.
Agent: Near Trinity College, you say?
Oleg: Yes. It's for me and a friend.
Agent: OK. Do you have any pets?
Oleg: No, we don't.
Agent: And are either of you smokers?
Oleg: No. Oh, and we'd like a place with a garage, too. My friend has car.*
Agent: And how much rent are you looking to pay per month?
Oleg: Not more than €1,400. That's our limit.
Agent: OK. I'll just have a look at what we have. One moment, please.

↪ ***Did you notice?***
Oleg says *My friend has car*. A native speaker would say *My friend has a car*.

💿20 (Agent = Irish; Oleg = Russian)
Agent: Hello?
Oleg: Yes. Did you find anything?
Agent: Well, there's one at 1,200 a month in Ivy Court. That has two bedrooms and a bathroom.
Oleg: Hmm. I know Ivy Court. Do you have anything closer to the city centre?
Agent: There's one in Joyce Street, but that has three bedrooms. It's 1,400. Oh, and one on North Foley Road, too, at 1,250. They all come furnished.
Oleg: OK. I would like to take a look at the last one, I think.
Agent: Fine, when would you like to see it, then?

💿21 (Property agent = American)
Yeah, well, the rent for this one is $795 per month. It's payable one month in advance, on the first of each month. We also need a deposit equivalent to six weeks' rent. This is refundable at the end of your tenancy, less any breakages or damage which you are liable for, of course. Bills such as gas, electricity and telephone are not included, so you need to set those up yourself.

💿22 (Property agent = American)
a If you want to move on before the end of the lease, then you need to tell us in writing at least one month beforehand.
b Buildings insurance is included, but not contents insurance.
c No. The rent can only increase after the term of your tenancy has expired.
d If the washing machine breaks down or anything like that, then call us out and we will send someone to repair it at no charge.
e It's for a year. That means twelve full calendar months, starting at the beginning of the month you move in.
f Absolutely not. You cannot rent out any rooms. If you do, you will break the terms of your tenancy agreement and you can be evicted.

💿23 (Lucy = Australian; Samir = Egyptian)
Mr Lee: Hello?
Lucy: Mr Lee. It's Lucy again.
Mr Lee: Oh, yes?
Lucy: I'm afraid I'm still waiting for someone to come and fix the cooker. Do you know how long it will take?
Mr Lee: I don't know. I haven't found anyone yet.
Lucy: What? This is an emergency. I can't cook anything!
Mr Lee: I'll try to find someone.
Lucy: It's been three days now. I'm not very happy about this at all.
Mr Lee: OK, OK. I'll get someone to fix it today.

Mr Lee: Hello?
Samir: Mr Lee?
Mr Lee: Yes.
Samir: I'm Samir … at 23 Cavendish Lane.

Mr Lee: Oh, yes. I was going to call you. Has the man been to fix the washing machine yet?

Samir: No, it's still broken. I told you about this a week ago.

Mr Lee: I called the repair company and they said they would send someone round.

Samir: Well, nobody has been. I'd like to know what you're going to do about it.

Mr Lee: I'll call them again.

Unit 4

🔊 **24** (a = Spanish; b = American; c = Italian; d = South African; e = Japanese; f = Egyptian; g = Australian)

a   A friend gave me this for my birthday, but I'd like to exchange it for something else.

b   Do you have the receipt?

c   I bought this shirt yesterday. It was a bargain, reduced from €65 to €20.

d   I think this DVD recorder is faulty. I can't seem to record anything.

e   You can't use a credit voucher to buy anything that's in the sale.

f   How much is the extended warranty on this plasma TV?

g   We don't give refunds, I'm afraid.

h   It isn't under guarantee, so we can't really help you.

🔊 **25** (Maribel = Brazilian)

Assistant: Next, please.

Maribel: Hello. Yes, I'm afraid but there is a problem with this blouse.* I bought it last week.

Assistant: Right.

Maribel: I washed it once and it's shrunk.

Assistant: I see. Did you follow the washing instructions?

Maribel: Yes. I followed the instructions on the label.

Assistant: It's very unusual. This is the first problem we've had with a Ray Nichols blouse.

Maribel: Well, I'd like my money back, please. Here's the receipt.

Assistant: We certainly can't give you your money back, I'm afraid.

Maribel: What?

Assistant: We've never had any problems with this blouse shrinking in the past, and it's very popular.

Maribel: Well, what can you do about it?

Assistant: Nothing. I'm sorry. I think it must be a fault with your washing machine. We can't accept responsibility.

Maribel: Well, I'm sorry, but that's not good enough. I want to make a complaint.

☞ ***Did you notice?**

Maribel says *I'm afraid but …* A native speaker would say *I'm afraid that …*

🔊 **26**

A   I saw John today.

B   I saw John today.

🔊 **27** (3 and 4 = American; 5 and 6 = Australian)

1–6   Good morning. How are you?

🔊 **28** (Manager = South African)

Well, if the item is damaged or faulty, then as long as you bring it back in under two weeks, we'll refund or exchange it straight away – whichever you want. You need a receipt, of course. Or we'll repair it free of charge. If the problem is it's an unwanted present or something, then as long as it's less than two weeks after the purchase date, we will refund or exchange it. If it's longer than that, then we'll give you a credit voucher.

🔊 **29**

a   What size is the screen?

b   How long does the battery last?

c   Is this the latest model?

d   What's the picture quality like?

e   How big is the memory?

f   Can I plug it into my TV?

🔊 **30**

1   That's one of the best things about this model. It has a 30GB hard disk which can store up to 37 hours of video.

2   Yes, it's just come out on the market.

3   You'll get around three hours' continuous use before you need to recharge.

4   It's got a two and a half inch, colour LCD.

5   Yes. It'll run your photos and video. You need to buy a special cable, though.

6   It's fantastic. It's got twelve mega pixels, so it's really sharp and clear.

🔊 **31**

Yeah, we've got two great offers at the moment. The S340 – this one – is 4G, so it's got really fast Internet. You know, while you surf, you can download video clips and stuff. It's got a fantastic six mega pixel camera as well … It's on the front – here – so you get two-way video calling. Or we've also got this one … the 410i, which has a built-in MP3 player, and a radio, with stereo sound. You can store over 3,000 songs on it. It's also got a full keypad, so it's like a pocket PC. Oh, and it's got a huge ten gigabyte hard drive as well.

🔊 **32** (Pierre = French)

Pierre: This vase is great. How much is it?

Stallholder: That's thirty-five pound* to you, mate.

Pierre: Oh, it's a bit more than I wanted to pay. Is that your best price?

Stallholder: Well, I suppose I can knock a fiver off. Let's say thirty pound*, then. How's that?

Pierre: It's very old and there's a crack in it. Can't you do any better?

Stallholder: No. It's a bargain, I promise you.

Pierre: OK. How much for cash?

Stallholder: That is a cash price!

Pierre: Well, I'll give you £20 for it.

Stallholder: Oh, all right. It's a deal.

☞ ***Did you notice?**

The stallholder says *thirty-five pound* and *thirty pound*. This is part of his regional dialect. In standard British English we would say *thirty pounds*.

🔊 **33** (a = Chinese; c = Spanish; d = American)

a   You can have the desk for $45.

b   OK. You can have this Rolex watch for $390. How's that?

c   I'll sell this scarf to you for $10.

d   You can have all the glasses for $15. Do we have a deal?

e   The best I can do is $30 for the lot. That's the six cups and the plates as well.

Unit 5

🔊 **34**

Fiona: And now it's time to go to Matthew Jenkins, our very own movie critic, for news of an exciting new film … Matthew?

Matthew: Thank you, Fiona. Yes, *New Beginnings* is a heart-warming tale set in 18th-century England. It follows the life of Jane Martins, a maid in a large country house who falls in love with the dashing Charles Danton, the son of a wealthy farmer. The story is gripping from beginning to end and is well acted throughout by Helen Richards and Peter Kite. Thanks to the sensitive direction of Kevin Hadley, the whole film blends together well, leading to a very surprising but utterly believable finale. This film should bring Hadley the recognition he has deserved for such a long time. Without doubt, it's the must-see movie of the year. Great for all the family. Five stars.

🔊 **35** (1 = Russian; 2 = German; 3 = Spanish; 4 = Australian; 6 = American)

1   It really makes me laugh. I think the characters is so funny* and the animation is great too. It's a classic.

2   It's the only chance I get to find out what's been going on in the world and catch up with current affairs.

3   It's about all I watch on TV these days, actually. I mean, if it wouldn't be for the football* and the tennis, I don't think I'd have a TV at all!

4   Oh, I love it. I don't think I've missed a single episode. I try to guess who the murderer is at the beginning and I'm so good at it now, I'm almost always right!

5   I love trying to guess all the answers. It's good when people win a lot of money, too. I like that.

6   I don't know how they do it, but they always manage to capture the animals behaving really naturally and it's just like you're there yourself.

☞ ***Did you notice?**

1 The Russian man says *the characters is so funny*. A native speaker would say *the characters are so funny*.

3 The Spanish man says *if it wouldn't be for the football …* A native speaker would say *if it wasn't/weren't for the football …*

36 (a = Chinese; c = Egyptian; d = Indian; e = Brazilian)
a   Yeah, I didn't use to like it when it first started, but now I'm really into it.
b   No, I'm not very keen on it, really.
c   It's very well written and everything. The acting is totally convincing.
d   The plot is so ridiculous that I can't watch it.
e   Some of the jokes fall flat, but most are pretty funny.

37
Welcome to News 24. I'm Sandy Caulfield. Here are today's headlines … A report into the state of the world's economy predicts a downturn for European Union and North American economies, but says that China could become the dominant superpower by 2025. In other news, 15 Members of the European Parliament protest about inefficiency and waste at the EU's headquarters in Brussels … Why eco-tourism might not be so good for the planet after all, and how scientists in Germany found a 3,000-year-old mammoth. … In tennis, new star, Bill Matson, enjoys a surprising win over world number three, and why the future of Formula 1 may be in doubt.

38
But first, our main story. A report by experts at the Global Studies Institute predicts that China, once known as the world's sleeping giant, is fast catching up with the major world economies and may be the dominant economic superpower as early as 2025. Since China's economic reforms began back in the late 1970s, the country has enjoyed staggering success and commercial expansion. The report predicts Chinese companies will soon have up to 50% of the American market and 30% of the European market. Our Asia correspondent, Tim Robbins, reports from Shanghai …

39 (Announcer = American)
If you are one of those people who shares the common belief that older women cannot be good mothers, then think again. In a recent study at the University of Southern California, researchers compared the experiences of 150 mothers in their 30s, 40s and 50s. The results were perhaps surprising. It appears that women in their 50s do not find being a parent more stressful or physically more demanding than women in their 30s and 40s.

40
A group of top European and Australian scientists say that temperatures will rise much faster than previously predicted, possibly by as much as six per cent by the end of the century. They also say that the record loss of sea ice over recent years means that the earth may no longer be able to recover.

41
Dr Mark Welles, from the University of Columbia, says that the evidence for global / warming is undeniable. The warning signs have

been here for ages, but we / haven't done anything about it, he argues. Soon the polar ice caps will / melt. As a result, animals like polar bears will become extinct. Sea levels will / rise and more and more land will be lost to the sea. Hundreds of thousands of people will have to move / home, until finally the whole earth will be / underwater. It's OK for people alive today, but it will be a big, big problem / for our children and the generations to come.

Unit 6

42 (Mohammed = Egyptian)
Doctor: Hello, Mr … ?
Mohammed: Mohammed. Mohammed El Metwalli.
Doctor: Please take a seat. Now, what seems to be the trouble?
Mohammed: I've got a terrible pain in my shoulder.
Doctor: I see. Do you know when it started?
Mohammed: About three days ago, I think.
Doctor: Oh, dear. Well, I'd better take a look. Now, where does it hurt exactly?
Mohammed: Just here, in the middle of my shoulder, at the back.
Doctor: Right. Is it painful if I do this?
Mohammed: Yes, it hurts a lot.
Doctor: Are you allergic to anything?
Mohammed: No, I don't think so.
Doctor: Hmm. Have you got any other symptoms?
Mohammed: Yes, I have a bad headache and I feel too dizzy.*
Doctor: Have you been taking anything for it?
Mohammed: No, I haven't. I wanted to see a doctor first.
Doctor: OK. Well, the first thing I want to do is take your temperature and then we'll do a full examination.

☞ *Did you notice?
Mohammed says *I feel too dizzy*. A native speaker would say *I feel very dizzy*.

43 (Doctor = Indian)
Conversation 1
What seems to be the trouble? a
Do you know when it started? b
How long have you been feeling like this? c
What symptoms have you got? d
Are you feverish? e
Have you been taking anything for it? f

Conversation 2
What seems to be the trouble? a
Where does it hurt exactly? b
Do you know when it started? c
Is it painful if I do this? d
What about if I do this … here? e
Have you been taking anything for it? f

44 (Doctor = Indian)
What seems to be the trouble?
Do you know when it started?
How long have you been feeling like this?
What symptoms have you got?
Are you feverish?

Have you been taking anything for it?
Is it painful if I do this?
What about if I do this … here?
Have you got any other symptoms?
Do you know if you are allergic to anything?

45 (Doctor = South African)
Doctor: Good afternoon.
Sharon: Hi there.
Doctor: What seems to be the trouble?
Sharon: Well, I've got these red blotches all over my legs … See? Here … and here.
Doctor: Oh, yes. I see. Are they painful?
Sharon: No, not at all. But they seem to be getting bigger.
Doctor: How long have you had them?
Sharon: About a fortnight now, I suppose. And there's a rash, too, on my arm.
Doctor: Oh, yes. That looks quite angry. Have you been scratching it?
Sharon: Yes, it's really itchy. What do you think is causing it?
Doctor: Well, are you allergic to anything? Cats, for example?
Sharon: Not that I know of.
Doctor: Hmm. Do you feel stressed?
Sharon: Well, yes. I suppose I do. I've been very busy at work for quite a while, but …
Doctor: Well, that might be it.
Sharon: What? Are you saying that this is because of stress?
Doctor: I think it could be. I'll give you a prescription for a cream. It's quite good, so in a few days the blotches should start to go, and the rash should clear up too.
Sharon: Good. Thanks a lot.
Doctor: Here you are. Come back and see me in a couple of weeks if it doesn't get better.

46 (Dr Vasquez = Spanish; patient = American)
Dr Vasquez: OK, so I think you are coming down with the flu.
Patient: No, really?
Dr Vasquez: Yes. Antibiotics are no use, of course, as it is a virus, so I recommend aspirin to relieve the aches and pains, and nausea, of course. And you should drink lots of water and stay in bed.

47 (Dr Vasquez = Spanish; patient = American)
Patient 1
Dr Vasquez: You have a chest infection, I'm afraid.
Patient: Oh, dear. Really? Are you sure?
Dr Vasquez: Yes. I don't think it's too serious, though.
Patient: Thank goodness for that!
Dr Vasquez: But you'll have to take some antibiotics. Take two, twice a day. Once in the morning and again at night, for five days.
Patient 2
Dr Vasquez: Well, I think you have a mild case of asthma. It's not too serious, so don't worry, but I want you to use an inhaler whenever you feel short of breath. Come and see me next week and we'll see how you are.

Patient 3

Dr Vasquez: I think this is a very bad cough. I'll prescribe some strong cough medicine. Take two spoonfuls every three hours. It will make you tired, so don't drive. Come back in three days and we'll see if you're better.

🔊 **48** (Dr Vasquez = Spanish)

a   I think you're suffering from a migraine. I'll give you a prescription for some tablets that are very good. Take two tablets, three times a day before meals. It should be better in a day or two.

b   Well, I think this is food poisoning. You need to drink lots of water and avoid alcohol or coffee. Don't eat anything until you start to feel better, and then have simple food that's easy on the stomach, like rice and chicken. Oh, and have small portions.

c   For insomnia, it's often a matter of getting more exercise and avoiding eating too much, especially at night. Don't drink alcohol and have some warm milk before you go to bed.

🔊 **49** (c = Australian; e = American; f = Brazilian; g = Indian; h = Canadian)

a   My blood pressure is very high.
b   My asthma has almost completely gone.
c   I always get terrible hay fever in summer.
d   We both got very bad sunburn on holiday.
e   I have finally gotten over my insomnia.*
f   I usually get a migraine after eating chocolate.
g   The doctor said my leg is not broken after all.
h   It looks like I'll need another operation.

↻*Did you notice?
In American English people say *gotten*.
A British English speaker would say *got*.

🔊 **50**

I'll give you a prescription.
The operation was a success.

🔊 **51**

a   Are you allergic to anything?
b   Come back at the end of the week and we'll see if you're better.
c   It's not serious, so I don't want to give you any tablets.
d   The exercise will help you a lot, so please do it.
e   Who is your regular doctor?
f   You are quite ill, I'm afraid.
g   The good news is that we aren't going to operate.
h   Your knee is a lot better now.

Unit7

🔊 **52** (2 = American; 3 = American; 4 = Brazilian; 5 = Canadian; 6 = French)

1   Oh, my ideal holiday is … you know … relaxing on the beach, swimming. And the kids love playing in the sea, making sand castles, of course!

2   I really like looking around museums, going to cathedrals and that kind of thing. Hopping on a sightseeing bus. You know, just exploring.

3   Oh, it's the best. Catching the cable car to the top of the mountain and then zooming down with all the fantastic scenery in front of you … You can't beat it.

4   I need lots of things to do … Fun things, like mountainbike riding – that's my favourite – or canoeing, and I like horse-riding too. Holidays are for doing exciting things.

5   I love being outdoors, you know, like waking up in a tent and then going fishing all day.

6   It's great because you just sit on the deck and relax, look out to sea and wait for the world to come to you!

🔊 **53** (Travel agent = South African)

Travel agent: Hello. Take a seat. How can I help?
Simon: We're thinking of going to Canada, Vancouver and then to Calgary.
Jenny: Yes, flying to Vancover on June the 12th.
Travel agent: OK. How many nights?
Jenny: Just eight. Coming back on the 20th, from Calgary.
Travel agent: OK … just a moment … Yes, with Air Canada, that'll be £780 per person, including all taxes.
Jenny: Oh, that's better than we thought!
Simon: Hmm! We were thinking three nights in Vancouver first. Somewhere rather nice?
Travel agent: We have a special on at the moment with the Metropolitan. It's a lovely hotel, four stars … You can see it here. That's, um … £140 a night.
Jenny: Per person?
Travel agent: No, that's for the room. All these are per room per night, without breakfast.
Simon: Oh, yes. It certainly looks very nice.
Travel agent: It is! I stayed there last year. And you should definitely hire a car – it's only £30 per day for a small car – and drive to Lake Louise.
Jenny: Oh, yes. We want to go there.
Travel agent: I recommend you stay at the Emerald Lake Lodge. It's a perfect place to explore from.
Simon: That sounds good.
Travel agent: Let me see … that'll be £150 per night. It's worth spending two nights there.
Simon: Two nights?
Travel agent: Yes, it's a nine-hour drive from Vancouver, so two nights is best. And then you can drive to Jasper – that's four hours. Two nights at the Fairmont Jasper Park Lodge will be £250 per night. It's expensive, but it's well worth going there. A beautiful place.
Simon: Look, a log cabin!
Travel agent: Yes. You get your own cabin.
Jenny: And there's plenty to do in Jasper National Park, is there?
Travel agent: Sure. You can play golf, go hiking … and boating if you fancy that. Then you've got a five-hour drive to Calgary. A final night somewhere like the Westin will save money – just £74. There's enough for a day – shopping, museums and Calgary Tower,

of course. You can drop your car off at the airport and fly back at ten in the evening.
Simon: Well, that's the kind of thing we were thinking of, isn't it, dear?
Jenny: Yes, it is. Can you print out those details and we'll take a brochure?

🔊 **54**

a   Can you recommend a good place to stay?
b   Is it worth hiring a car?
c   Do you know a nice place to eat?
d   Where can I change money?
e   What's a good way to spend an evening?
f   Where are the best places to go shopping?

🔊 **55** (Tour guide = Indian)

Do you want to go on a night cruise? a
Just two hours. b
We'll pick you up by bus outside the hotel. c
At six o'clock tomorrow night. d
Bus to and from the hotel, and the cruise. e
Dinner isn't included, but you get one free drink. f

🔊 **56** (Speaker = American)

a   What range of cars do you have?
b   Is insurance included?
c   Do I have to pay an excess if I have an accident?
d   Can I hire a car one-way?
e   Is there a mileage limit?
f   Do you provide child car seats?
g   Is accident cover included?
h   What documents do I need?

🔊 **57** (Speaker = German)

1   If you average more than 250 miles per day, then there's a charge of €10 per mile.
2   We have all kinds: small, compact, mid-sized and full-sized.
3   Sure. There's an extra charge of €30 for all one-way hires.
4   Yes, full cover is provided for every named driver.
5   Yes, all that's covered. There's a 24-hour emergency number to call if you need assistance.
6   You need a valid driver's licence or an international licence with a passport.
7   Yes, you have to pay the first €900 of any claim.
8   Yes. They're free of charge. We'll fit them for you in the back seat.

🔊 **58** (Laura = Italian; assistant = Irish)

Laura: I'd like to hire a car for a week, from next Monday.
Assistant: Certainly. What class of car would you like to have?
Laura: Em, well. What have you got?
Assistant: Our Economy car is a two-door Polo. That's 89 euro for a week.
Laura: Hmm. That's too small. We are four.* Do you have anything else?
Assistant: Next up is a Compact car. A Ford Fiesta. The rate for that is 99 euro.
Laura: Is that an automatic?
Assistant: No, it's manual.

Laura: I want an automatic, really. What automatics have you got?
Assistant: We have a Toyota Corolla. Let me see … that's 139 euro for the week.
Laura: Wow. That's a big increase.
Assistant: Yes, well, it's a bigger car. It's an Intermediate class. All our full-sized cars are automatic, too, but they're 169 euro.
Laura: Oh, I see.
Assistant: Actually, we have a special offer on at the moment. I think we have an automatic Corolla … Yes, for 125 euro.
Laura: OK. That's the one!

☞ *Did you notice?
Notice that Laura says *We are four*. A native speaker would say *There are four of us*.

🔊 **59**
Why doesn't she rent the Ford Fiesta?
Did he say he'd have the car for next week?

🔊 **60**
a   I've got just one question.
b   You didn't say you couldn't swim.
c   We could go tomorrow.
d   You must be tired.
e   Have you played before?
f   I managed to talk to her last night.
g   Are you taking him to the station?
h   I didn't know the answer, so I kept quiet.

Unit8

🔊 **61** (Emmanuel = French)
Mark: Hi, Emmanuel? Have you got a minute?
Emmanuel: Of course, Mark. What is it?
Mark: Well, I'm going to Paris for a few days next week … and as you're from Paris, I was wondering if you could give me some tips? You know, where to go and stuff like that.
Emmanuel: Of course! Have you found anywhere to stay?
Mark: Not yet. I'm still looking. It's quite pricey.
Emmanuel: Well, try the Latin Quarter. That's a very historic part of the city, and it should be quite reasonable. It's really lively, too, because it's the students' area.
Mark: Sounds good, thanks. What about getting around?
Emmanuel: That's easy. Just use the Metro. It's usually quite crowded, but it doesn't cost much. Or you can walk, of course. You can see almost everything that way …
Mark: OK, and what is there to see?
Emmanuel: Oh, there are so many things. You should definitely see the *Arc de Triomphe*. And if you like big cathedrals, then you must to go to *Notre Dame**, of course, and …
Mark: It's euros in France, right?
Emmanuel: Yes. When I go, I usually just use my bank card and get cash from ATMs. It's no problem.
Mark: Is it safe?

Emmanuel: Yes, it's as safe as London or any other city, I think. Just be careful in the main touristy places.
Mark: OK, thanks, Emmanuel. That's a great help.

☞ *Did you notice?
Emmanuel says *you must to go to Notre Dame*. A native speaker would say *you must go to Notre Dame*.

🔊 **62** (Guide = Spanish; tourist = German)
Guide: Welcome, everyone, to lovely Lima! Lima is called Ciudad de los Reyes, or the City of Kings. This is where the Spanish founded the city, in 1535 … and for almost 300 years, Lima was the centre of Spanish rule in Latin America. And today, it is Peru's capital city.
Tourist: Sorry, can I ask a question?
Guide: Yes.
Tourist: What about the Incas? They were here before the Spanish, weren't they? Could you tell us a bit more about them?
Guide: Yes. In fact, there were many Inca towns here when the Spanish arrived, and over 400 temples and palaces, but it was the Spanish who actually founded the city of Lima, right here, in this square, on the site of an existing palace. This is Plaza Mayor, the main square. It is now a World Heritage Site … You are now standing on the exact site where Francisco Pizarro founded the city nearly 500 years ago. You can see the Government Palace, where the President lives …
Tourist: Sorry to interrupt, but these buildings don't look 500 years old.
Guide: That's right. An earthquake in 1746 destroyed almost all of the city. Only 20 buildings were left. You can see San Francisco's Convent over here … that's the only building in Plaza Mayor that survived. Now, let us to walk* over here …

☞ *Did you notice?
The guide says *Let us to walk over here …* A native speaker would say *Let's walk over here …*

🔊 **63**
He told us a bit about when the Spanish arrived in Peru.
An earthquake destroyed almost all of the city.

🔊 **64**
a   Can I take a brochure, please?
b   We got on the boat and sailed across to the island.
c   I want a table with a view of the sea, if possible.
d   I had a good look around the castle.
e   We went out with a group of friends that afternoon.

🔊 **65** (Guide = Spanish)
a   It was the Spanish who actually founded the city of Lima. … Of course, go ahead.

b   The most fashionable shops are in Miraflores, which is a busy area of the city near … No problem. What do you want to ask?
c   These days Barranco is the liveliest district of the city, with lots of restaurants and bars. … Yes, what is it?
d   There are, of course, lots of festivals and celebrations throughout the year and … OK. What is your question this time?
e   The traffic in Lima has got worse, of course, in recent years, but the city is taking measures to … I'd rather you let me finish, if that is all right.

🔊 **66** (Speaker = Brazilian)
a   That's the Modern Art Museum, the most popular one in the city, and on the left …
b   A big festival we have here in the city is Mardi Gras, but there are others such as …
c   Lord Byron stayed at that hotel over there on the corner and up ahead we can see …
d   This is the exact spot where the old castle used to be and over there is …
e   There are two palaces here: the National Palace and the Pena Palace. The Pena Palace is the most famous. You can see …

Review 1

🔊 **67** (3 and 4 = Indian; 7 and 8 = Egyptian; 9 and 10 = Chinese)
1   I don't really like horror films.
2   Have you made a reservation?
3   You can have the camera for £30.
4   That film's terrible. Don't bother watching it.
5   I guess I'd better be going.
6   Is it worth hiring a car?
7   I'd be interested to hear more about your holiday.
8   I saw Simon yesterday.
9   I don't suppose you know anywhere good to stay in London?
10   What seems to be the trouble?

🔊 **68** (5 and 6 = Russian; 7 and 8 = German)
1   a   Excuse me. Where can I pay?
      b   Sorry, but we've been waiting for our drinks for ages.
      c   I can't eat this. I'm allergic to nuts.
2   a   You may be right, but it doesn't work.
      b   I told you a week ago this printer was broken.
      c   I'm afraid this printer has broken. I've only had it a week.
3   a   OK. I'll buy it. It's a deal.
      b   No, really. It's my treat.
      c   I know what you mean, but I can't.
4   a   I'd like to know what you're going to do about it.
      b   Where does it hurt exactly?
      c   Is it OK if I don't come in today?
5   a   I was wondering if I could go there.
      b   It's well worth going there.
      c   It's not worth it.
6   a   Thank goodness for that!
      b   It was nice talking to you.
      c   I'm sorry. That's not good enough.

7 a I'd like to know more about the museum.
  b Have you heard more about the museum?
  c I'm afraid that I don't know any more about the museum.
8 a What's up?
  b See you later.
  c I haven't seen you for ages.
9 a Well, what a relief!
  b Thank goodness for that!
  c Oh, no. That's terrible.
10 a I should take the tourist bus.
   b Do you think it's a good idea to take the tourist bus?
   c Is it OK if I take the tourist bus?

CD2 Work and Study

Unit 9

2 (Vicky and assistant = American)
Assistant: Hello, Johnson's Office Solutions. Can I help you?
Vicky: Oh, hello. This is Vicky, from Kelta & Co. We've got a problem with our photocopier.
Assistant: I see. Did you purchase it from us?
Vicky: Yes, we did.
Assistant: And is it still under warranty?
Vicky: We got a three-year extended warranty. It's only a year old.
Assistant: OK. And what seems to be the trouble?
Vicky: The paper's jammed and we can't fix it.
Assistant: Right. Did you look in the manual?
Vicky: Yes. I've had a go, but I still can't fix it.
Assistant: All right. I'll have a look and see what we can do. Hmm … we can't get anyone there until late afternoon, I'm afraid.
Vicky: I'm sorry, but that's no good at all. We're very busy here and we need this fixing immediately.
Assistant: Hmm. Well, I can see if … Oh, yes. It looks like we might be able to get someone to you this morning.
Vicky: OK. What time will they be here?
Assistant: I can't say exactly. Any time between 10.30 and 12. Is that OK for you?
Vicky: Well, I suppose so. If that's the best you can do. At least it's this morning.

3 (b = American; d = Chinese; e = Brazilian; f = Spanish)
a We have the books you ordered. When would be a good time to drop them round?
b I can come sometime next week. What day would suit you best?
c We can come on Friday afternoon to install your broadband connection. Is that OK?
d I'd like to see you next Thursday. What time would suit you best?
e So, what about a meeting sometime later this month? What date is good for you?
f We can't come today, but tomorrow after four looks possible. Would that be convenient?

4
a I'm sorry. We won't be able to repair it for at least four weeks.
b I'm afraid we can't send anyone until tomorrow afternoon.
c Oh, yes. Your light. It will be another fortnight before we can replace that.
d We don't have any heaters in stock. I've got no idea when we'll get any more.
e No, we can't send anyone to help you. All the lads are out at the moment.
f John is away on holiday and won't be back for two weeks, I'm afraid. There's really not very much we can do before then.

5 (Stuart and Melanie = Australian)
Stuart: So, do we have a deal?
Melanie: Well, the price is much higher than last year.
Stuart: But that includes all the extras I told you about … and the free upgrade to our Gold Plan. Remember, that gives you 24-hour cover, and free antivirus protection.
Melanie: Yes, but …
Stuart: Don't you see that this service agreement means all the workstations here will be covered all day, every day. That's over thirty computers.
Melanie: Yes, but they are very reliable anyway, mostly.
Stuart: But it only takes one problem to cause a disaster.
Melanie: Yes, I see what you mean, I suppose.
Stuart: You won't find more comprehensive coverage for less. Or better service.
Melanie: It's just I don't know if we can afford it.
Stuart: Are you sure that you can afford *not* to take out this cover? … Look, I'll tell you what I'll do. If you agree now, I'll give you a five percent discount. How's that? Don't you agree that that's a great deal?
Melanie: Five percent?
Stuart: That's right. I can't do any better than that. Now, what do you say?
Melanie: Hmm. Well … I'll need some time to think this over.

6
Is that your best offer?
You'll have to do better than that, I'm afraid.
If you order now, we'll give you a discount.
We might be able to come down on price if you order in bulk.
I'll give ten percent extra free provided that you sign a one-year contract.

7
A: OK, so if I pay in advance, you'll give me a ten percent discount?
B: Yes, and if you pay now, then I'll give you a fifteen percent discount.

8 (A = American)
a A: If we agree to the deal, we will lose control of the company.
  B: Yes, but if we don't agree to the deal, the company will collapse.

b A: If we increase our prices, we will make more profit.
  B: Yes, but if we decrease our prices, we will get more customers.
c A: If we move production to Asia, costs will go down.
  B: Yes, and if we don't move production to Asia, we will be uncompetitive.

Unit 10

9 (a = French; b = Saudi; c = American; d = Italian; e = Australian; f = Russian; h = German; i = Japanese; j = Indian)
a Hello. I'd like to open an account, please.
b My chequebook's run out. Can I order a new one, please?
c Can I check my balance, please?
d I'd like to pay this cheque into my current account, please.
e Can I send some money abroad from here?
f I want to deposit this money into my savings account.
g Can I pay my electricity bill here?
h I'd like to buy some traveller's cheques, please.
i Could I see someone to arrange an overdraft, please?
j I need to order a new bank card. I've lost mine.

10
1 Yes, of course. I'll need to see some form of identification, such as your passport, or driving licence … and proof of your address, so a utility bill with your name and address.
2 Oh, dear. Well, I can certainly order a replacement for you here, but you need to telephone our 24-hour emergency number to report it, if you haven't done that already.
3 Yes, of course. Can I have your paying-in slip and your bank card, too, please? Do you have a Regular Saver or a Bonus Saver account?
4 Yes, you can, but utility bills take seven working days to go through. Is that all right?

11 (Raymond = Chinese; bank clerk = Canadian)
Raymond: I'd like to open a savings account, please.
Bank clerk: Certainly. Which type of savings account do you want?
Raymond: Er, what do you have?
Bank clerk: Well, if you have a lump sum to invest, I'd recommend our First Reserve account. That has an interest rate of 3.5%, paid annually, but you must have at least $5,000.
Raymond: No, I was thinking of saving around $100 a month, actually.
Bank clerk: OK, so our Bonus Saver account might be better. That has an interest rate of 3%. Interest is paid every three months.
Raymond: Can I take the money out if I need it?
Bank clerk: Yes, but you must give 30 days' notice before you can make a withdrawal.
Raymond: Oh, I see. Actually, I want an account where I can get at the money immediately.

Bank clerk: Then you should have our Regular Saver account. It's instant access. The rate is 2.3%. Interest is paid monthly, but there's a penalty if you take money out.

Raymond: What do you mean by 'penalty'?

Bank clerk: Well, if you withdraw money, then you won't get any interest for that month.

Raymond: Oh, I see. Do you have an internet savings account?

Bank clerk: Yes, we do. That's our e-Savings account. The interest rate is 4.1%. It's paid every month. You have to save at least $75 every month. Our e-Savings account is instant access, too.

Raymond: Does that mean I can get at the money immediately?

Bank clerk: Yes, and there's no penalty.

Raymond: Maybe I'll have that one, then.

Bank clerk: You have to apply online for that. We can't do it here in the branch.

Raymond: OK. Well, thank you very much for your help.

12 (b = American; c = Irish; e = Indian)

a   The interest rate is 3% but, if you have over £25,000 invested, then it goes up to 3.5%.

b   This is a three-year bond and the amount you invest is locked away for the whole term.

c   There are no charges on this account, except for the administration fee of €295.

d   Our usual interest rates are around 4 to 5% unless you have an online account, which pays 9%.

e   This is a fixed interest account.

13 (a = American; d = Chinese; e = American)

a   This account has a variable rate of interest. … Variable means the interest rate can go down or up.

b   All our loans are secured on your property. … That means we have a legal right to take the money from your property if you don't repay.

c   There is a minimum balance of £3,000 with this type of account. … That means you have to have at least £3,000 in the account at all times.

d   You can only invest a lump sum in this account. … A lump sum means a single, one-off deposit, rather than regular deposits.

e   We also offer an automatic fee-free overdraft of $1,000 with online accounts. … That means you don't have to ask for an overdraft up to $1,000, and you don't pay anything for the facility.

14 (b = South African; e = American; g = French; h = Indian)

a   Can I have a £20 top-up voucher, please?

b   Could you send off my application for a driving licence, please? I've filled in the form and this is my ID.

c   I'd like to pay my electricity bill, thanks. Here it is.

d   Could I have £150 in Canadian dollars, please?

e   I'm moving house next week. Can you send my mail to my new address?

f   I want to collect my pension, please. This is my card.

g   Here's £200. I need to send this to France, please.

h   Can I have a £10 phone card, please?

15 (Brigitte = Swiss)

Brigitte: Hello. I'd like to send this package to Switzerland.

Clerk: Can you put it on the scales, please? OK, so that's about 1.3. That'll be £5.28 by surface mail. It should be there in under two weeks. What's in it, anyway? A present?

Brigitte: No, some brochures and ten promotional DVDs. It's for a colleague. How long will it take by airmail?

Clerk: Airmail will take three days. I'll just check the price … Oh, £5.89. Not much difference.

Brigitte: Oh, well, I'll send it airmail then. Is it safe? I mean, this is quite important.

Clerk: Well, if you want a signature when it's delivered, you can send it International Signed For. That's an extra £3.50, so that'll be £9.39.

Brigitte: I see.

Clerk: Or, for an extra £4.20, you can send it Airsure. That means priority handling and online tracking for the whole journey. It's the most secure way to send it, and faster, too. It takes two days. That'll be £10.09. Switzerland is outside the EU, so you have to fill in a Customs label. Are the total contents less than £270?

Brigitte: Oh, yes. The brochures are, say, £10 and the DVDs cost about £3 each to make, I guess.

Clerk: Then fill in this CN22 label and stick it on the top left, can you?

Brigitte: Sorry? Could you say that again?

Clerk: Complete this label and put it on the top left corner.

Brigitte: Oh, right. I'll send it by the last way you said. The quickest.

Clerk: Airsure? Fine.

16

A: OK, so if I send this by International Signed For, it'll get there in two days?

B: No, it'll get there in three days. If you send it by Airsure, it'll get there in two days.

17

a   A: So I have to fill in a CN22 Customs label?
    B: No, you need to fill in a CN23 Customs label.

b   A: So I fill in a VN1 form and then go to the Payment section?
    B: No, go to the Payment section first and then you can fill in a VN1.

c   A: Did you say it will take two weeks by standard mail?
    B: No, it'll take three weeks by standard mail. It'll take two weeks if you send it Swiftmail.

Unit 11

18 (Wen Ling = Chinese)

Wen Ling: Oh, hello. Is this where I report something stolen?

Guard: Yes, that's right. Just let me get the right form …. OK, what's your name, please?

Wen Ling: Wen Ling Tsai. That's W-E-N space L-I-N-G Tsai … T-S-A-I.

Guard: OK, and where do you live?

Wen Ling: 17a Park Avenue, Bristol. The postcode is…

Guard: Whoa, hang on! 17a Park Avenue, you say?

Wen Ling: Yes, in Bristol. The postcode is BR2 6YT.

Guard: 6-Y-T … OK. So, what was stolen?

Wen Ling: My bag. I was outside the library. This man just grabbed it and ran away.

Guard: I see. So, when was this?

Wen Ling: At around 12.30.

Guard: OK. Did you get a look at him?

Wen Ling: Yes. He was medium height with short dark hair and glasses. Oh, and he had a moustache.

Guard: Right. And what was he wearing?

Wen Ling: Blue jeans and a black jumper, I think. And white running shoes.

Guard: OK. Now, additional details. Can you describe the bag?

Wen Ling: It's a small, black leather bag, with a zip along the top and a shoulder strap.

Guard: Are there any distinguishing marks on it? Any scratches, for example?

Wen Ling: Not really. Just a small tear on the handle.

Guard: OK, well, we'll look into it.

19 (Hassan = Syrian)

Operator 1:   Emergency. Which service do you require?

Hassan: Oh, er, ambulance, I think. There's been an accident.

Operator 2:   Go ahead, caller. You're through to the ambulance service. Where do you need the ambulance to come to?

Hassan: Er, I'm not sure. There's a park. Hang on, there's a sign near the gate … I'm at Green Park.

Operator 2:   What's happened?

Hassan: There's been a traffic accident. A car has hit a cyclist, and he's on the ground.

Operator 2:   How many people are hurt?

Hassan: Well, the car driver's standing by the car. He's holding his head. I can see some blood, and the cyclist is on the ground next to me. There's no blood, but he isn't moving. There's nobody else here … I didn't know what to do.

Operator 2:   OK, stay on the line. An ambulance is already on its way. Now, I want you to …

🔊 20

a
Emergency. Which service do you require? …
Go ahead, caller. You're through to the ambulance service. Where do you need the ambulance to come to? …
What has happened there? …
How many people are hurt? …
Stay on the line. An ambuance is on its way. …

b
Emergency. Which service do you require? …
Go ahead, caller. You're through to the fire service. What is your name? …
Where are you calling from? …
Where is the fire? …
Is anyone trapped or injured? …
A fire engine is on its way. …

🔊 21 (Hassan = Syrian)

Police officer: What exactly did you see?
Hassan: I was walking past the park heading towards the city centre when a cyclist passed me and then a car came round the corner from the right, there. I don't know, I guess the driver didn't see the cyclist …

🔊 22 (Hassan = Syrian)

Police officer: How fast was the car travelling?
Hassan: Not very fast. Normal speed.
Police officer: So how did the car hit the cyclist?
Hassan: I think the cyclist was in the middle of the road to turn right, down where the car had come from, but I couldn't see any lights on their bike.
Police officer: What about the car?
Hassan: Er, well, the car had lights on. Yes.
Police officer: Was the car on the wrong side of the road?
Hassan: No.
Police officer: So the collision happened here?
Hassan: Yes, that's right. Right next to me. There was a big crash and then silence. I saw the cyclist in the road, unconscious, and the driver got out holding his head, so I phoned 999.

🔊 23

I was walking past the park, heading towards the city centre.

🔊 24

a   How fast was the car travelling?
b   So the collision happened here?
c   There was a big crash and then silence.

Unit 12

🔊 25 (Kenji = Japanese)

Kieran: Hello. This is Kieran Donnelly speaking.
Kenji: Oh, er, hello. Is James Green there?
Kieran: No. I'm afraid he's out of the office right now. I'm his personal assistant. Would you like to leave a message?
Kenji: Er, yes, thanks. I was supposed to meet him at two o'clock this afternoon, but something has come up. I wonder if we can

rearrange it to 4 pm instead, and maybe meet here in my office, that's in Building 3, rather than in the main building?
Kieran: OK, so … meet in your office in Building 3, not the main building, at four o'clock, not two. Got it.
Kenji: Thanks.
Kieran: OK. I'll make sure he gets that. What's your name, please?
Kenji: Kenji Fujita. That's K-E-N-J-I Fujita, F-U-J-I-T-A.
Kieran: OK. And does he know what number to contact you on if there's a problem?
Kenji: He's only got my cell phone number. My office number is 0207 772994. That's direct.
Kieran: Sorry, what was that last part again, please?
Kenji: 772994. Oh, and can you please to ask him* to call me before one thirty to confirm? I'll be in a meeting after that.
Kieran: Will do.
Kenji: OK. Thanks very much.
Kieran: You're welcome. Thanks for your call.

☞ *Did you notice?
Kenji says *Can you please to ask him* … A native speaker would say *Can you please ask him* …

🔊 26 (b = American; c = South African; d = New Zealand; e = Australian)

a   Can you say that I'll be about thirty minutes late? If she wants to start the meeting without me, that's fine, because I can't guarantee exactly when I'll be there. The traffic's terrible.
b   Tell her I can't find the blue file, that's the one with the sales figures for this month. I need it urgently because I have to prepare for tomorrow's meeting.
c   Please can you tell her that Tina from Accounts called? I need to have a completed expense form from her by Friday lunchtime or she won't get her expenses back this month.
d   Please tell her I've managed to change her flight from 10am to 3.30, and a taxi will pick her up outside her apartment at midday. When she arrives in Paris, Mr Wilkinson will be there to meet her.
e   Can you say the best price we can do is $1,500. That's including delivery and free installation. We need an answer tomorrow morning by eleven at the latest or she'll lose the order.

🔊 27 (b = Spanish; c = Japanese; d = American; e = Australian)

a   Yes, please. Tell her Mr MacGregor called, would you?
b   I think that's everything. Oh, and say she can reach me on Extension 349 if she needs to.
c   So the meeting will be at the hotel next Friday in the Baker Suite.
d   And her flight number is TX743.
e   … and please say I can't process his order without written authorization and either Form VS901 or VS942a, depending on the insurance classification.

🔊 28 (Hilda = German)

Kieran: Hello. This is Kieran Donnelly speaking. How may I help you?
Hilda: Hello. This is Hilda Birghard calling. Can I speak to James Green, please?
Kieran: I'm afraid Mr Green is out of the office right now.
Hilda: Would you mind taking a message?
Kieran: Not at all.
Hilda: Can you tell him that the report he asked for on next year's marketing strategy it is almost ready,* but we have a couple of queries we need answering first.
Kieran: OK, so … queries for the marketing strategy report. Sorry, I didn't get your name.
Hilda: Hilda Birghard. B-I-R-G-H-A-R-D.
Kieran: Thank you. So, there are two queries, you say?
Hilda: Yes, the first is what percentage of his clients are what we call 'valued customers' … that means they have ordered from the company before, and what is their average age? Have you got that?
Kieran: Yes, OK. Got it. And the second?
Hilda: How many sales resulted from last summer's television campaign, and what was the net income compared to the cost?
Kieran: Sorry, what was that last bit again?
Hilda: What was the net income compared to the cost? Does that make sense?
Kieran: Fine. I'll make sure he gets this when he gets in. It should be mid-afternoon sometime.
Hilda: OK, that's great. Thanks very much.

☞ *Did you notice?
Hilda says … *it is almost ready*. A native speaker would say … *is almost ready*.

🔊 29

a   Could I leave a message, please?
b   Thanks a lot. I appreciate it.
c   Does that make sense?
d   Do you think you could take a message?
e   Can I ask who's calling?
f   Have you got that?
g   Who is this, please?
h   Would you mind taking a message?
i   I appreciate your help. Thank you.
j   Sorry. I didn't get your name.
k   Could you repeat that back?

🔊 30

Do you think you could take a message?

🔊 31

a   Would you mind taking a message, please?
b   I'm afraid he's not in today.
c   I think he said he'd managed to do it.
d   I'll call her if there's a problem with the order.
e   I'd appreciate it if you could say I'll be late.

Unit 13

🎵 **32**
a   I think so too.
b   Do you see?
c   Could you say what you mean?
d   Let's move on, shall we?
e   It's a deal.
f   Yes, I agree.

🎵 **33**
a   I think you're absolutely right.
b   That's not right at all.
c   I think we're drifting off the point a bit.
d   Right, now let's move on, shall we?
e   Can you explain what you mean by that?
f   Could I come in here, please?
g   Let's get down to business, shall we?
h   What's your opinion on this?

🎵 **34** (Julie = American)
Catherine: OK, so let's get started, shall we? The first item on the agenda is what are we going to do about the decline in sales? We have to do something. I'd like to start by asking Mark.
Mark: Well, we might consider spending more money on marketing.
Catherine: Hmm. Julie, do you have any thoughts?
Julie: I think that's a good idea. More marketing means more sales.
Peter: Sorry, can I come in here?
Catherine: Yes, Peter. Of course.
Peter: I couldn't disagree more with Julie and Mark. Marketing is expensive, and we have no guarantee that the costs will be worth it. Perhaps you can give us your opinion, Catherine?
Catherine: Yes, well, I can see where Mark and Julie are coming from, but I have a problem with increasing our marketing budget for the same reason that Peter has just given. We can't be sure of the results. I propose we hire a new sales manager. How do you feel about that, Mark?
Mark: That sounds reasonable to me. I think some new blood would be a good thing.
Julie: I have no problem with that, either.
Catherine: So, Mark and Julie both think it's a way forward. Peter?
Peter: Well, I'm afraid that's not how I see it, Catherine. Again, it means trying to spend our way out of this crisis and I'm not very keen on that idea at all.

🎵 **35**
I'd like to start by asking Celaya.
Carol, do you have any thoughts?
How do you feel about that, Miguel?
Perhaps you can give us your opinion, Mr Tanaka?
Mustafa, what's your reaction?
Jenny?

🎵 **36** (c = French; d = Indian; f = American)
a   Could we perhaps spend more money on marketing?
b   How about hiring a new sales manager?

c   We might consider sacking some employees.
d   I suggest we do some market research.
e   Why don't we reduce our prices?
f   I propose we try to expand our market.

🎵 **37**
Do you think we should go ahead?
Is everyone happy with that decision?
What do you think we should do?
Who's going to take responsibility for this?

🎵 **38**
a   Does everyone agree?
b   Is that your final answer?
c   Where are the sales figures?
d   Why are the results so poor?
e   Do you think the situation will improve?
f   Does this price include delivery?
g   Who's the new marketing manager?
h   Have you finished the report yet?

🎵 **39** (b = Spanish; c = Egyptian; d = Japanese; e = Brazilian)
a   So, I guess that means you're happy with the sales figures.
b   You said you believe output will improve next year.
c   You mean that we shouldn't launch in February?
d   If I understand you correct,* you think our investment has been a mistake.
e   So you're saying you'll never agree to the plan.

☞ ***Did you notice?**
The Japanese woman says *If I understand you correct*. A native speaker would say *If I understand you correctly*.

🎵 **40** (a = American; b = Indian; c = French)
a   OK, so before we finish, let me just summarize the main points. All managers are to get a ten percent bonus, in line with contractual agreements, and the sales force is to double within six months. Right, I think we've covered everything, so shall we call it a day?
b   And now I'll quickly go over today's main points. We all agree that the new product is a success. That's good. But there are some reliability issues we need to tackle and also pricing. If we do that, I am sure it will be too profitable.* Good. So it looks like we can finish early today.
c   Er … to sum up, then, it seems we need to start a programme of staff redundancies. This will probably begin next spring. Now, we'll have to cut this meeting short, I'm afraid. I have some urgent business to attend to …

☞ ***Did you notice?**
The Indian woman says *it will be too profitable*. A native speaker would say *it will be very profitable*.

Unit 14

🎵 **41**
Extract 1
Here at the Engineering Department we pride ourselves on our health and safety record, so first I want to run through a few basic safety measures you need to observe while you are here with us. First, always wear a laboratory coat and any additional protection, such as safety goggles or shoes where necessary. Second, there is no smoking anywhere on the premises, of course, and also, no food or drink. Third, keep all doors and windows closed …

Extract 2
We have recently updated and improved all our resources and equipment. We have also developed new teaching approaches, so now lectures and project work are more integrated than previously.

Extract 3
One main area of interest here, both theoretical and in its practical applications, is the area of sustainable energy technologies. We are world leaders in research into the best use of the world's natural resources and in pioneering engineering solutions to climate change.

🎵 **42** (Lecturer = American)
The figures are staggering. We are emitting four times as much carbon today than we were just ten years ago – despite the Kyoto agreement. In the early 19th century, levels of carbon dioxide in the atmosphere were 280 parts per million. Today they are 380 parts per million. It may not mean much to you, but let's look at the consequences …

First, as ice in Greenland and Antarctica melts – and it is melting far faster than anyone had predicted, by the way – as the ice melts, sea levels will rise, possibly by as much as six metres. Flooding will affect millions of people living in coastal areas all around the planet. Huge populations, entire cities, will have to move to higher ground. Second, heat waves will become more common, with tens of thousands of people dying from heat, and from the wild fires that will sweep across the planet in the dry conditions. In the rising temperatures, severe droughts will mean crops fail, so millions more will starve to death. We don't have to look far into the future to see this. Just a few years from now, a recent study estimates that as many as 300,000 people a year will die directly as a result of global warming … and that's not counting the impact on animals, birds and fish.

So, what can we do? In all this despair, is there any hope? Well, if we take action individually, we can collectively make a huge difference. There are plenty of things we all can do to fight global warming. First, recycling. Recycle everything you can and buy recycled goods. Second, think about your food. Buy fresh food, not frozen food. It costs ten times more energy to produce frozen food. And buy locally grown produce, too. Did you know the average meal in the US has travelled 1,200 miles to get on your plate? Third, save energy. You can save up to 30 percent of the energy you use by doing simple things like turning off the light if you are not in the room, and using long-life light bulbs, which are 60 percent more efficient than normal light bulbs. Use the air-conditioning less, wash your clothes at a lower temperature if possible, don't use a dishwasher, turn off electronic appliances when you are not using them … So, we can all save energy very easily. And fourth, transport. Don't take a car – use public transport, or even better, walk or cycle. If you have to use a car, do so as part of a car pool and take others. Even just checking the tyres are inflated correctly will make a three-percent saving in efficiency.

Yes, there are many things you can do. And there are many things governments can do too. Did you know there are over 200 separate environmental agreements? Sounds impressive, doesn't it? Until you realize all of them are hard to enforce and poorly coordinated. Each government needs to pass effective laws to force individuals and industry to take responsibility for climate change.

The fact is, we must do something. We are in the middle of a fight for the very survival of the planet here. Some people say it is too late already and that the planet is doomed to die … We are not at that point yet, but it's not far away. Now, let's look at …

43 (Lecturer = American)
a   The solution, then, is in the hands of everyone here.
b   Unless governments act decisively and together, there will be a global disaster.
c   There will be more and more problems, such as drought, starvation, flooding …
d   So should we just sit back and do nothing about this? Leave it to someone else? No!
e   As long as we all try to do what we can, then there is a chance the planet will survive.

44 (Lecturer = American)
Yes, there are many things you can do. And there are many things the government can do too. Did you know there are over 200 separate environmental agreements? Sounds impressive, doesn't it? Until you realize all of them are hard to enforce and poorly coordinated. Each government needs to pass effective laws to force individuals and industry to take responsibility for climate change.

Unit 15

45 (Stephanie = American)
Good afternoon, everyone, and welcome. Today I'm going to talk about job prospects for graduates. I'll start by describing the current position for graduates leaving university. Then I'll look at salaries, and what you can expect. After that, I'll move on to career choices, and show the most popular choices of career that graduates select, and finally, I'll review the main points covering what employers look for when they are recruiting graduates. We'll have time for questions at the end.

46 (Speaker = Russian)
Well, that's all I have to say about our sales and marketing strategy. I hope you all agree with the direction we're taking. Now I would like to turn to our overseas operations, where I see a lot of potential for growth and expansion, especially in China and the Far East. To give you an example of how important Asia is to our business, I want you to look at this graph which shows that when we go to Asia …

47 (Speaker = Canadian)
OK, so I've told you about our pensions policy. As I say, I see some tough times ahead, but I think we'll get through them. Let me now turn to staff recruitment, which is an area of particular concern. We have been losing too many experienced staff. A good example of this is in the Accounts department, where last month alone three of our most senior staff resigned.

48 (Speaker 1 = American; speaker 2 = Australian)
Speaker 1:   Good afternoon, everyone. Today I'm going to talk about Sasco Systems, its future, and … anyway, to start with, I'll describe the current financial position of the company. Then I'll mention some of the new projects we have started this year. After that, I'll move on to the opportunities we can see for further expansion, together with some of the difficulties we might anticipate. Finally, I'll review …
Speaker 2:   All in all, the results so far have been very encouraging and the future looks equally bright. In conclusion, then, based on the figures I have shown you, we can safely say the company is set to go from strength to strength. Right, let's stop there. Thank you all for listening. I've enjoyed it and I hope you have too. Now, does anyone have any questions?
Speaker 3:   So, yeah, er … next I want to show you this graph, um … of the figures for this financial year. You can see that we've had a great year, and everything looks to be progressing as expected. There was a ten percent rise in sales overall, and, yeah, this was what we pretty much expected, so, moving on, this slide shows another one and um, great …

49 (Stephanie = American)
To sum up briefly, then, the future for graduates looks very bright indeed. There are more jobs, and salaries are increasing. I hope this comes as good news to you all as you approach the end of your time here at college. Thank you all for listening. Remember that you can ask either myself or anyone here in the careers centre for advice at any time. Now, does anyone have any questions?

50
Summarizing the main points
a   To sum up briefly, then, …
b   I'd like to review the main points …
c   In conclusion, then …

Thanking your audience
d   Thank you all for listening.
e   Thank you very much for your attention.
Inviting questions
f   Now, does anyone have any questions?
g   Can I answer any questions?
h   Are there any final questions?

51 (Stephanie = American; Student 2 = Indian; Student 3 = Japanese; Student 4 = Brazilian; Student 5 = Chinese)
Stephanie: Remember that you can ask either myself or anyone here in the careers centre for advice at any time. Now, does anyone have any questions?
Student 1:   Yes, I have a question.
Stephanie: Sure. Go ahead.
Student 1:   When did you carry out this survey?
Stephanie: Between early February and the end of March this year.
Student 2:   Excuse me?
Stephanie: Yes? Please ask your question.
Student 2:   Who exactly did you ask?
Stephanie: We asked hiring managers. That is, those people within a company that recruit new employees.
Student 3:   Er, can I ask a question?
Stephanie: Yes, of course. What would you like to know?
Student 3:   How many people did you ask?
Stephanie: We asked hiring managers in more than 1,000 companies. Now, does anyone else have a question?
Student 4:   Yes, I have. How did you do the survey? I mean, was it by mail?
Stephanie: That's a good question! Actually, it was quite easy. We did it all by email. We emailed everyone direct and attached an online survey.
Student 5:   Yes, I have a question. How do employers … [fade]

52 (a = Egyptian; b = Italian; c = American; e = Canadian)
a   Excuse me. Can you explain that last point in more detail?
b   Sorry, but can you tell us how did you conduct the research?*
c   Don't you agree that the restructuring programme is a costly waste of time?
d   Do you think we can get enough sales without spending more on marketing?
e   What would happen if the two case studies were reversed?

↻*Did you notice?
The Italian woman says *Can you tell us how did you conduct the research?* A native speaker would say *Can you tell us how you conducted the research?*

Unit 16

53 (Greg = New Zealander)
Right, well, er … my talk today is on learning styles. I chose this because there is a lot of research into it and it seems as if nobody really agrees on how to assess learning styles. I'll start by outlining some competing theories about

how people learn … There aren't any handouts, I'm afraid, but anyway … One theory is the VARK system. That was a theory by … I can't remember now, but V-A-R-K means V for visual, A for auditory, like hearing, R for reading and K for, I don't know how to pronounce this … kinaesthetic? K-I-N-A-E-S-T-H-E-T-I-C. Yes, that's it. Kinaesthetic. That means things like touch, movement and stuff. Anyway, according to the VARK system, depending on your learning style, you learn in different ways. If you're a visual learner, then you need to use charts and pictures, use colour highlighting in your notes, and stuff. If you're an auditory learner, then reading aloud and listening will help you learn. Reading is just reading, of course. You learn by reading. Kinaesthetic learners need to move around while they learn. You're a kind of hands-on person if you're that kind of learner, according to the VARK system, so you should revise while standing up and walking around the room, for example. Anyway, that's just one theory. There are lots of others too, for example …

54 (Greg = New Zealander)
So, to conclude then, personally I think that we all have our own learning style and we are not just one type or another. In other words, we are probably a blend of lots of styles. I don't think any of the learning styles I've told you about is better than any other. I think the problem is that we all learn in different ways, and trying to find a system to fit in all the different ways we learn, it just doesn't work. We are too creative to be boxed in like that. Not everything about the human brain can be mapped and predicted. How we learn is different for each person, so the point I'm making is I don't know how useful it is to try to categorize everyone into types.

55
Speaker 1:   OK, well, now I'd like to move on and talk to you about the next item, which I think is the most interesting. Basically, what I'm saying here is that I think the situation over the next few years will really improve …
Speaker 2:   OK, well, now I'd like to move on and talk to you about the next item, which I think is the most interesting. Basically, what I'm saying here is that I think the situation over the next few years will really improve …

56 (Greg = New Zealander; Students A and B = Australian; Student C = Japanese)
Greg: So, that's basically what I want to say about this for now. Are there any questions?
Student A: Er, yes. I have a question. You say that most people are multimodal, in other words they have several learning styles. Is that good?
Greg: I think it's unavoidable. We don't just learn in one way. We learn in many ways.
Student A: Yes, but that's not really what I was asking. I meant, what do you think are the advantages of being multimodal?

Greg: Oh, I see. I think the main advantage is flexibility, you know. We don't rely on just one way to learn. And we can learn in many situations, in many ways. It's definitely a strength, being multimodal.
Student B: I'd like to ask about VARK …
Greg: Sure.
Student B: I think it was Fleming who came up with VARK. Some people say a learning style should have 18 or more dimensions, you know, like light, heat, food and so on … Isn't VARK just about how we process information?
Greg: There are many aspects to how we learn and depending on which you emphasize then they are called a learning style. As I said, I don't think one is better than another. They're all different.
Student B: I think you've answered a slightly different question. What I want to know is, do you think VARK is a learning style?
Greg: Well, I think it is, yes, because it informs our view of how we learn.
Student C: Do you think learning styles are fixed or can they change? Can we develop new learning styles as we get older, for example?
Greg: Oh, I think each person's learning style can change, but certain basics do not. So if you are a visual learner in VARK's system, you will always be a visual learner. I guess what I'm saying is you don't lose a learning style, you just adapt and use others in different times.
Student C: Do you think there are any gender differences? You know, do men and women learn in the same way?
Greg: I think there are no differences, actually.
Student C: I disagree. I think men and women learn quite differently. In VARK, men are more kinaesthetic, for sure.
Greg: Well, I don't know. I haven't really studied that part in detail. But knowing what your learning style is helps you be a better learner, for sure.

Review 2

57 (3 and 4 = Indian; 9 and 10 = Chinese)
1   We can give you free delivery if you pay in advance.
2   That was a long message. Did you understand everything?
3   Could we reschedule the meeting to Friday?
4   Now, does anyone want to ask a question?
5   So you're saying that the report will be finished tomorrow?
6   Shall we say three o'clock tomorrow afternoon?
7   When shall I give you a ring?
8   Did you get through to Paul?
9   Who is this, please?
10   I think you're absolutely right.

58 (5 and 6 = Russian; 7 and 8 = German)
1   a   You can't expect us to wait that long.
    b   I don't see it like that at all.
    c   Do you mind if we press on?
2   a   I don't get what you mean.
    b   I think I've got that.
    c   That's fair enough.
3   a   Would you like to leave a message?
    b   Can I take a message?
    c   Would you mind taking a message?
4   a   What do you mean exactly?
    b   I'm sorry. I didn't quite catch that.
    c   Sorry, that's not quite what I meant.
5   a   Do you mean you are leaving the company?
    b   You can't expect me to believe that.
    c   Right. I think I've got that.
6   a   OK. I think I've got that.
    b   What about three o'clock?
    c   Did you say three o'clock?
7   a   Hang on. I'll just put you through.
    b   Would you like to leave a message?
    c   Sorry. The line's engaged.
8   a   Sorry. Can you run that by me again, please?
    b   Can you explain what that means?
    c   Repeat, please.
9   a   Perhaps my question wasn't very clear.
    b   Right, now let's move on, shall we?
    c   I'll deal with questions at the end, if that's OK.
10   a   Hello, everyone, and welcome.
    b   I'd like to review the main points.
    c   I'll try to answer any questions you may have.

Answerkey

Unit 1

Get ready to listen and speak

○ 1 How's it going? How are you doing? What's up?
2 I guess I'd better be going. Right, I must dash. It was nice talking with you.
3 See you around. Have a nice weekend. Talk to you later.

A

1 2 c   3 a   4 b
2 Hi there. What's up? How are you doing?
3 1 Morning. Hey! Long time no see.
2 Right, I'm off! It was lovely to see you. I should get going, I suppose. It's been great to talk with you.
3 Take care. Bye!

B

1 a No, they're meeting for the first time.   b They work in a hotel.
2 b False (She works in Housekeeping.)   c True, d False (He's been there three years.)   e Don't know f True g Don't know,
h Don't know

C

2 b Me too.   c Me too.   d Me neither.   e Me neither.
f Me too.   g Me neither.   h Me neither.   i Me neither.   j Me too.

D

2 *Your own answers. Possible answers*:
b What do you do? Do you like your job? Where exactly in New York do you work?
c What's wrong with it? Have you taken it to be repaired? Have you had it long?
d Where did you get it from? How much was it? Did you buy it for yourself?
e Where are you going to do that? When are you going to start? Why do you want to do that?
3 *Your own answers. Possible answers*:
b That's great. Did she have a boy or a girl? Have you been to see her yet?
c So, why don't you do much sport these days? What sports did you use to do? Are there any sports you still play?
d Oh, dear. Why not? When was the last time you saw them? Where do they live? Did you fall out?
e What do you want to go there for? Are you going to go shopping? Who are you going to go with?

E

1 2 d 3 e 4 a 5 f 6 c
2 2 Disagree 3 Agree 4 Disagree 5 Agree 6 Disagree
3 Expressions to agree with someone: I couldn't agree more. I think so too. Definitely.
Expressions to disagree with someone: That's not right at all! No way! I don't agree. I don't think so.

F

1 b 5 c 1 d 2 e 3
3 *Your own answers. Possible answers*:
a I know what you mean, but we still need politicians.
b I may be wrong, but these days it seems many people don't think so.
c Yes, but there are many places where it's legal.
d You may be right, but I think it's mainly the media that gives us that impression.
e I agree to some extent, but it depends how much overtime you do.
4 *Your own answers. Possible answers*:
b I agree to some extent, but perhaps they need the money so they have to work.
c I know what you mean, but you can get a better job if you have a degree.
d I may be wrong, but if taxes are lower the government won't be able to pay for things like schools and hospitals.
e Yes, but computers are so useful it's hard to manage without one.

Unit 2

Get ready to listen and speak

○ *Your own answers.*
○ *Your own answers.*

A

1 b During the meal c Before the meal d Before the meal
e During the meal f Before the meal g During the meal
h During the meal
2 b 4 c 5 d 8 e 7 f 1 g 3 h 6
3 2 ready to order
starter
main course
anything to drink
3 dessert
the bill

Focus on describing food

Positive adjectives: tender, crispy, juicy, fresh, tasty
Negative adjectives: bland, greasy, tough, underdone, overcooked
Your own answers. Possible answers:

salty – bacon   hot and spicy – curry   sour – vinegar
sweet – sugar   bitter – lemon   savoury – chicken
steamed P F   sautéed P   baked P F   medium S
roast P   fried S P F   well-done S   mashed P   boiled P F
grilled S F   (stir / deep)-fried P F

B

1 Ravioli Filberto, Pollo Toscano, Bistecca al Norte, Tiramisù
2 b Ravioli Filberto   c Bruschetta   d Pollo Toscano
   e Bistecca al Norte

Sound smart

2 rese<u>rva</u>tion   p<u>o</u>tato   pas<u>ta</u>   star<u>ter</u>   pop<u>ular</u>

C

2 *Your own answers. Possible answers*:
   No, you paid last time. Let me get it. / I'll pay this time. / It's my turn.
   No, I'll pay. Really, I insist. / Please let me pay.
   Of course. It's my pleasure. / Yes, I'd like to. / Yes, it's my turn.
   You're welcome. / No problem. / Don't mention it.

D

1 b 3   c 4   d 1   e 6   f 2
2 a Excuse me.   b I'm afraid …; Sorry, but …
4 *Your own answers. Possible answers*:
   b Sorry, but I've been waiting for my main course for twenty minutes.
   c Excuse me. I'm afraid I don't like this wine. I think it might be 'corked'.
   d Sorry, but these vegetables are under-cooked.
   e Sorry, but I think this bill is wrong. I've been charged too much.
   f Excuse me. I asked for sparkling mineral water, but this is still.
   g Sorry, but I asked for green salad and this has tomato in it. I'm allergic to tomato.
   h Sorry, but this glass of mineral water is warm. Can I have some ice?

E

1 The Big Bistro: Service – Good, Food quality – Poor, Value for money 6/10
   Sala Thai: Atmosphere – Good, Service – Good, Food quality – Good, Value for money 9/10
2 The Big Bistro:
   Staff: professional
   Service: very attentive
   Food: disappointing (tuna salad unimaginative, steak rather tough, potatoes under-cooked)
   Cost: £25
   Sala Thai:
   Atmosphere: relaxed and inviting
   Staff: very friendly
   Service: excellent
   Food: absolutely delicious (soup very enjoyable, fish very tasty)
   Cost: £20

Unit 3

Get ready to listen and speak

○ b 4   c 3   d 1   e 2
○ modern P   spacious P   cramped N   comfortable P   private P
   shabby N   quiet P   bright P   noisy N   messy N   isolated N
   dingy N
○ *Your own answers.*
○ *Your own answers.*

A

1 a He's going to share with a friend.
   b He wants to rent.
2 b flat   c near Trinity College   d two   e two   f No   g No
   h a garage   i €1,400
3 74 North Foley Road

B

1 b 2   c 5   d 3   e 1
2 To ask about alternatives:
   a <u>Do you have anything</u> with a larger garden?
   b <u>Is there anything</u> away from the main road?
   c <u>Don't you have anything</u> cheaper?
   To express a preference:
   d <u>I'd rather</u> have something near a better school.
   e <u>I'd prefer</u> something closer to the city centre.
3 *Your own answers. Possible answers*:
   b I'd rather have something that's in a quieter area, if there is anything.
   c I really like the house, but it doesn't have a garden. Don't you have anything with a garden?
   d I'd prefer to have something with a garage. It's very important.
   e Is there anything a bit cheaper? That's too expensive for me.

Focus on comparatives and superlatives

b the most expensive   c better   d nearer   e as large as
f more convenient

C

1 The agent covers all the questions.
2 a $795 per month.   b On the first of each month.   c Equivalent to six weeks' rent.   d Yes.   e No.

D

1 1 e   2 c   3 b   4 f   5 a   6 d
2 b True   c True   d False (Repairs are no charge.)   e False (It starts from the beginning of the month you move in.)   f False (You *can* be evicted.)

E

1 a Is it OK if I …? Would you mind if I …? I was wondering if I could …
   b Could you …? Would you mind …ing?
2 *Your own answers. Possible answers*:
   b Is it OK if I get satellite TV?
   c Would you mind if I changed telephone company? I'm not very happy with the one I'm with at the moment.
   d Is it OK if I buy a new sofa? I don't want the old one so it needs to be taken away.
   e I was wondering if I could have broadband Internet installed? I'll pay, of course.
3 *Your own answers. Possible answers*:
   b The window in my bedroom is broken. Would you mind replacing it?
   c The heating doesn't work properly. Could you get it fixed, please?
   d Would you mind getting someone to tidy the garden? It's a mess.
   e Could you repair the front doorbell, please? It doesn't work.

Answer key

F

b Three days ago.
c To get someone to fix it today.
d The washing machine doesn't work.
e A week ago.
f To call the repair company again.

G

1 Lucy says *I'm not very happy about this at all.*
Samir says *I'd like to know what you are going to do about it.*
2 *Your own answers. Possible answers:*
  b I told you two weeks ago that the smoke alarm was broken, but nobody has been to repair it yet. I'd like to know what you are going to do about it.
  c The gardening hasn't been done for two months and it looks terrible. I'm not very happy about this at all. When are you going to send someone to do it?
  d The kitchen sink has been blocked since last week. Please can you tell me what you are going to do about it? I'm not very happy about this at all.
  e Last night I saw a mouse in the kitchen. I really must insist that you do something about this immediately. It's very urgent.

Unit4

Get ready to listen and speak

- b 6 c 4 d 1 e 7 f 8 g 5 h 3
- a Customer b Shop assistant c Customer d Customer
  e Shop assistant f Customer g Shop assistant
  h Shop assistant

A

1 b It shrank after only one wash. c She asks for her money back.
  d Because she thinks there is no fault with it. She thinks Maribel washed it incorrectly. e Maribel decides to make a complaint.
2 Purchased: Last week
  Receipt: Yes
  Problem: Item has shrunk (only washed once).
  Action taken: No refund or credit voucher given.

B

3 *Your own answers. Possible answers:*
  b Sorry, but the radio I bought last week has stopped working.
  c I got this vase for my birthday, but I'm afraid it's cracked.
  d I bought these shoes two months ago and I'm afraid that they're already falling apart.
  e I'm sorry, but my new tennis racquet broke the first time I used it.

> **Sound smart**
>
> 2 2 bored 3 worried 4 friendly 5 angry 6 tired

C

b True c True d False e True f True

D

1 b 6 c 5 d 6 e 5 f 7
2 b How long does the battery last?
  c Is this the latest model?
  d What's the picture quality like?
  e How big is the memory?
  f Can I plug it into my TV?

3 A digital camcorder.
4 a 4 b 3 c 2 d 6 e 1 f 5
5 b video c Six d Two-way e radio f 3,000 g keypad h Ten

E

1 b Let's say 30 pound, then. How's that?
  c It's a bargain, I promise you.
  d That is a cash price!
  e It's a deal.
2 b best price c do d for cash e I'll give

F

2 *Your own answers. Possible answers:*
  b No, I can't pay that. Is that your best price? c OK, that's fine. It's a deal. d Sorry, it's too much. I'll give you $10. e That's OK with me.

Unit5

Get ready to listen and speak

- *Your own answers.*
- b horror c science fiction d war e thriller f fantasy
  g action h love story i western j animation
- *Your own answer.*

A

1 Charles Danton – The son of a wealthy farmer, Helen Richards – The actress who plays Jane Martins, Peter Kite – The actor who plays Charles Danton, Kevin Hadley – The director
2 b Don't know c True ('well acted throughout') d False ('gripping from beginning to end'), e False ('this film should bring Hadley the fame and recognition he has deserved for such a long time.') f False ('Great for all the family'.)

B

1 Positive: well acted, lots of twists and turns, very surprising, gripping, utterly believable, original
  Negative: too long, a bit boring, predictable
2 heart-warming, gripping, well acted, very surprising, utterly believable

C

1 2 news 3 sport 4 crime series 5 quiz show 6 nature
2 1 characters, funny, animation 2 find out what's been going on, current affairs 3 football, tennis 4 episode, murderer
  5 guess the answers, win a lot of money 6 animals behaving really naturally
3 b N c P d N e P
4 b I'm not very keen on it. c well written, totally convincing
  d ridiculous e pretty funny

D

1 Six
2 politics, the environment, science, sport
3 – 15 MEPs protest about inefficiency + waste at the EU's HQ (Brussels)
  – Eco-tourism may not be good for the planet
  – Scientists in Germany find a 3,000-year-old mammoth
  – Tennis star Bill Matson beats world number three
  – Future of Formula 1 may be in doubt
4 b No ('is fast catching up'). c By 2025. d In the late 1970s.
  e 50%. f 30%. g The programme's Asia correspondent.

E

1 c

2 *Your own answer. Possible answer*:

It's about older women being mothers. A report by the University of Southern California found that mothers in their 50s don't find being a parent more stressful or physically demanding than younger mothers.

F

1 *Your own answers.*

2 scientists, temperatures, rise, century, loss, sea ice, recover

3 The underlined words are the words actually spoken. However, your answer doesn't need to be exactly the same, but similar.

Dr Mark Welles, from the University of Columbia, says that the evidence for global <u>warming is undeniable</u>. The warning signs have been here for ages, but we <u>haven't done anything about it</u>, he argues. Soon the polar ice caps will <u>melt</u>. As a result, animals like polar bears will become extinct. Sea levels will rise, and more and more land will <u>be lost to the sea</u>. Hundreds of thousands of people will have to move <u>home</u>, until finally the whole earth will be <u>underwater</u>. It's OK for people alive today, but it will be a big, big problem <u>for our children and the generations to come</u>.

Sound smart

2 Dr Mark <u>Welles</u>, from the University of <u>Columbia</u>, says that the <u>evidence</u> for global warming is <u>undeniable</u>. The <u>warning signs</u> have been here for ages, but we haven't done anything about it, he argues. <u>Soon</u> the polar ice caps will <u>melt</u>. As a <u>result</u>, animals like <u>polar bears</u> will become <u>extinct</u>. Sea levels will <u>rise</u>, and <u>more and more</u> land will be <u>lost</u> to the <u>sea</u>. <u>Hundreds</u> of <u>thousands</u> of people will have to <u>move home</u>, until <u>finally</u> the <u>whole earth</u> will be <u>underwater</u>. It's OK for people alive <u>today</u>, but it will be a <u>big, big problem</u> for our <u>children</u> and the generations to <u>come</u>.

Unit 6

Get ready to listen and speak

○ *Your own answers. Possible answers*: a stomachache, a backache, a cold, the flu, a cough, a temperature, a toothache, an earache

○ b 2 c 4 d 3 e 1 f 6

○ *Your own answers.*

A

1 2 know 3 hurt 4 painful 5 allergic 6 symptoms 7 taking

2 b About three days ago.

c He has a bad headache and he feels dizzy.

d No, he hasn't.

e He wants to take Mohammed's temperature and then do a full examination.

Focus on describing health problems

Words to describe a cough: tickly, chesty

Words to describe a pain: stabbing, dull, shooting

b runny c sore d bleed e sprained f temperature g feverish h numb i rash j blotches k itchy

---

B

2 *Your own answers. Possible answers*:

Conversation 1

b Yes, it started yesterday. c I've been feeling like this since yesterday morning. d I've got a runny nose, a sore throat and a headache, as well. e Yes, I feel a little feverish. f Yes, I've been taking some aspirin.

Conversation 2

a I've got a really bad pain in my back. b At the bottom, just here. c I think it started last Sunday. d No, it's not painful. e Yes! That's very painful. It hurts a lot. f Yes, I've been taking some pain killers.

3 *Your own answers.*

4 *Your own answers. Possible answers*:

a I've got a bad cough and a runny nose. I have a temperature and my body aches all over. I'm quite feverish, too.

b I often get headaches, and sometimes I feel dizzy too. I've also got a rash on parts of my body.

c My stomach aches very badly and I have diarrhoea. I feel nauseous, too.

C

1 c

2 a She has red blotches on her legs, and a rash on her arm.

b The doctor thinks it's stress.

3 b True (they are getting bigger) c True (about a fortnight ago)

d True (it's really itchy) e False f False (the doctor prescribes a cream) g True (in a few days) h False (only if it doesn't get better)

D

1 a He's coming down with the flu.

b Because the flu is a virus, so antibiotics aren't any use.

c Dr Vasquez advises the patient to take some aspirin (to relieve the aches and pains and nausea) and to drink lots of water and stay in bed.

2

	Diagnosis	Instructions
Patient 1	a chest infection	two tablets twice a day for five days
Patient 2	a mild case of asthma	use an inhaler / come back next week
Patient 3	a very bad cough	take two spoonfuls every three hours / don't drive / come back in three days

3 a ✓ b ✗ Both alcohol and coffee should be avoided. The patient is told not to eat anything until they feel better (and then eat small portions). c ✓ ✗ The patient should drink warm milk before going to bed.

E

1 Concern: Oh, dear. Really?

Relief: Thank goodness for that!

2 Oh, no. That's terrible. C Oh, I'm sorry to hear that. C Well, that's good news. R Oh, dear. Really? C How awful! C Phew! R What a relief! R

3 *Your own answers. Possible answers*:

b Well, that's good news. c How awful!

d Oh, no! That's terrible. e Thank goodness for that!

f Oh, dear. Really? g What a relief! h Oh, I'm sorry to hear that.

Sound smart

2 b Come back at the /j/ end of the week and we'll see /j/ if you're better.

c It's not serious, so /w/ I don't want to give you /w/ any tablets.

d The /j/ exercise will help you /w/ a lot, so please do /w/ it!

e Who /w/ is your regular doctor?

f You /w/ are quite ill, I'm afraid.

g The good news is that we /j/ aren't going to /w/ operate.

h Your knee /j/ is a lot better now.

Answer key

- *Your own answers.*
- *Your own answers.*
- b 3 c 1 d 2 e 4 f 5

A

1 2 a city break 3 a skiing holiday
  4 an activity holiday 5 a camping holiday 6 a cruise

2 2: museums, cathedrals, sightseeing
  3: cable car, mountain, zooming, scenery
  4: mountainbike, canoeing, horse, exciting
  5: outdoors, tent, fishing
  6: deck, out to sea

B

1

TrailBlazers				**Customer Booking Information**	
Booking Ref:	9873459				
Client:	Mr & Mrs Carter				
Flights					
From London (LHR) to Vancouver (YVR)					
June 12th	AC855	Dep 12:30	Arr 14:25	**No. people:** 2	**Cost per person:** £780
From Calgary (YYC) to London (LHR)					
June 20th	AC852	Dep ~~23~~ **22**:00	Arr 01:55		
Hotels				**Cost (prpn / breakfast not included)**	
Metropolitan Vancouver 4*		No. of nights: ~~2~~ **3**		~~£160~~ **£140**	
Emerald Lake Lodge 4*		No. of nights: 2		£150	
Fairmont Jasper Park Lodge 4*		No. of nights: 2		£250	
Westin Calgary 4*		No. of nights: 1		~~£84~~ **£74**	
Car hire:	(Compact) ~~£25~~ **£30** per day				
This quote valid for 14 days.					

2 a Per room per night
  b Vancouver to Lake Louise – 9 hours, Lake Louise to Jasper – 4 hours, Jasper to Calgary – 5 hours
  c Jasper National Park: you can play golf, go hiking and go boating. Calgary: you can go shopping, and visit museums and Calgary Tower.

C

1 2 b 3 a 4 b 5 a 6 b 7 a
2 3, 5, 1
3 *Your own answers.*

b up c back d to e in f around g out of h off
i back

D

2 *Your own answers. Possible answers*:
  b I see. Where does it leave from?
  c What time does it leave?
  d What exactly is included?
  e Are there any hidden extras?
  f OK. Thank you. I'll think about it.

3 Possible questions include: Where exactly does it leave from? How long does it last? What exactly is included? Is there anything you have to pay extra for, except for parascending?

E
1 b insurance c excess d one-way e mileage f child car seats
  g accident h documents
2 a 2 b 4 c 7 d 3 e 1 f 8 g 5 h 6
3 b Compact c €99 d Intermediate e 139 f 169
4 b It's too small. c It's not automatic. d €125 e It's a special offer.

2 a I've go(t) jus(t) one question.
  b You didn'(t) say you couldn'(t) swim.
  c We coul(d) go tomorrow.
  d You mus(t) be tired.
  e Have you playe(d) before?
  f I manage(d) to talk to (h)er las(t) night.
  g Are you taking (h)im to the station?
  h I didn'(t) know the answer, so I kep(t) quiet.

- *Your own answers.*
- *Your own answers.*
- b have c work out d go on e travel

A

1 transport, attractions, money, safety
2 b True c False ('it doesn't cost much') d True ('You can see almost everything that way.') e False ('It's no problem.') f False ('it's as safe as London or any other city')
3 a In the Latin Quarter. b Because it's the student area.

b interesting, c vibrant, d popular, e beautiful, f expensive,
g international, h quiet, i fashionable, j historic, k dirty

B

1 I was wondering if you could give me some tips?
3 *Your own answers. Possible answers*:
  b I wonder if you'd mind giving me a bit of advice about the weather? What clothes should I take? Will it be cold?
  c Do you think you could tell me how best to get around the city? / I wonder if you'd mind telling me the best way to get around?
  d What about safety? I was wondering if you could give me some tips? / Do you think you could give me some tips?
  e I don't suppose you know the best way to change money? / Would you mind telling me the best way to change money?
  f I don't suppose you know anywhere good to eat? / I was wondering if you knew any good restaurants?
  g Do you think you could suggest a few places to go in the evening?
  h I was wondering if you knew any good shops to go to? / Do you think you could tell me where the best place to go shopping is?

C

1 <u>Is it worth</u> visiting the aquarium?
   <u>Do you think it's a good idea to</u> walk to the castle, or is it too far?
   <u>Would you recommend</u> going to the National Museum?

2 *Your own answers. Possible answers*:
   b Would you recommend going to the Science Museum?
   c Do you think it's a good idea to go to a dolphin show?
   d Would you recommend going on the Night Safari?
   e Do you think I should visit some temples?
   f Is it worth visiting Sentosa Island?
   g Would you recommend going to Chinatown?
   h Is it worth visiting the Botanic Gardens?
   i Do you think I should go to Little India?

D

1 *Your own answers.*
2 b 1535 c 400 d main square e 500 f earthquake
3 b Francisco Pizarro was the founder of Lima. c The President of Peru lives in the Government Palace. d Only 20. e San Francisco's Convent (the only building in Plaza Mayor that survived the earthquake).

> **Sound smart**
>
> 2 b We got on the boat and sailed across to the island.
>   c I want a table with a view of the sea, if possible.
>   d I had a good look around the castle.
>   e We went out with a group of friends that afternoon.

E

2 Sorry, can I ask a question? Sorry to interrupt, but …
3 *Your own answers. Possible answers*:
   b Excuse me. I have a question.   c I'm sorry, but could I ask a question?   d Sorry to interrupt, but …   e Could I interrupt for a moment?

F

1 Could you tell us a bit more about them?
3 *Your own answers. Possible answers*:
   b Excuse me. I'd be interested to hear more about Mardi Gras, if possible.
   c Sorry, I'd like to know more about why Lord Byron stayed there.
   d I'm sorry, but can you say a bit more about the castle?
   e Excuse me. I'd be interested to hear more about the National Palace.

Review1

1 1 b, 2 a, 3 c, 4 a, 5 b, 6 b, 7 c, 8 c, 9 a, 10 b
2 1 b, 2 c, 3 a, 4 c, 5 b, 6 c, 7 a, 8 b, 9 c, 10 b
3 1 b, 2 a, 3 c, 4 b, 5 c, 6 c, 7 a, 8 b, 9 b, 10 b
4 *Your own answers. Possible answers*:
   1 I think so too. / You don't really believe that, do you? / No way! I don't agree. / That's not right at all.
   2 It was great. I had a lovely juicy steak and the chips were crispy. / It wasn't very good. The vegetables were over-cooked and the lamb was too greasy.
   3 Oh, dear. Really? / Are you sure? / That's terrible.
   4 That's a lot more than I wanted to pay. / Is that your best price? / Can't you do any better? / I can't pay that. It's not worth that.
   5 I've got a terrible pain in my shoulder/arm/back. / I have a high temperature and I feel feverish. / I've got a rash on my arm and red blotches on my legs.

6 It was wonderful. / It's definitely worth going there. / It was packed, of course, but it's such a lively place. / It's a bit touristy in parts, but overall I loved it.
7 No, please let me. It's my treat. / OK, that's very kind of you. / No, let's split the bill.
8 Yes, there's a very good place on Park View Road. It's very friendly and it's not very expensive. You could try that. / It's worth booking early.
9 I'm sorry, but that's not good enough. / I'm not very happy about this at all. / I want to make a complaint.
10 Yes, I've been taking some antibiotics. Two tablets three times a day.

Unit9

> **Get ready to listen and speak**
>
> ○ b of c of d for e with
> ○ *Your own answers.*
> ○ b the Internet   c a meeting   d a file by mistake   e a faulty telephone

A

1 b One year ago. c The paper's jammed. d Yes, but she couldn't manage to fix it. e Late afternoon. f Between ten thirty and twelve.
2 professional
3 quite satisfied (Someone will come that morning so she doesn't have to wait too long. Her tone of voice indicates disappointment, and she says *If that's the best you can do* which suggests she had hoped someone could come right away.)

B

2 Any time between 10.30 and 12.
3 *Your own answers. Possible answers*:
   b Any time between two and four on Friday would be great.
   c Sometime after ten on Tuesday is OK for me.
   d What about Friday morning? Shall we say ten o'clock?
   e Sometime early next week would be fine. Any day before Thursday, if possible.
4 *Your own answers. Possible answers*:
   b How about Thursday? Sometime in the morning would be fine.
   c Don't you have anything a bit earlier? Sometime on Friday morning, perhaps?
   d Any time between eleven and one would be great.
   e Tuesday the 19th is fine. Any time in the afternoon.
   f Not really, but any time between three and four would be great.

C

1 I'm sorry, but that's no good at all.
3 *Possible answers:*
   b Sorry, but you have to do something sooner. It's turning on and off all the time and disrupting everyone in the office.
   c It's simply not acceptable to leave it that long. I've been waiting for five weeks already. Can't you replace it sooner?
   d But you can't expect me to work in the cold. It's freezing in here. I really must insist that you do something about this right away.
   e Sorry, but you can't expect me to lift all these boxes myself. They are far too heavy, and there isn't time anyway. They have to be at reception in 20 minutes.
   f But I really must insist that you fix the toilet quicker than that. It's been out of order for nearly a month and it's a five-minute walk to the nearest one that works. I'm very worried about the effect this is having on staff productivity.

D

1 a Stuart is trying to sell a service agreement giving coverage for computers in case they go wrong.
  b direct and rather pushy
  c pressurized
2 a The benefits are it offers 24-hour cover and free antivirus protection.
  b Over 30 (all the computers in the company).
  c A five percent discount for an immediate agreement.

Focus on conditionals

b will have / pay c don't decide / will be d won't buy / isn't
e Will you call / have f pay / won't charge

b As long as c after d When e if f until

E

3 a Is that your best offer? / You'll have to do better than that, I'm afraid. (or Is that the best you can do? as in the title of this unit)
  b If you order now, we'll give you a discount. / We might be able to come down on price if you order in bulk. / I'll give ten percent extra free, provided that you sign a one-year contract.
4 Your own answers. Possible answers:
  b If you pay in advance, we'll promise free delivery.
  c We might be able to offer free installation if you order two.
  d I'll give one-year free insurance, provided that you order in bulk.
  e I'll give you a 25% discount, provided that you sign a two-year contract.

Sound smart

2 a A: If we agree to the deal, we will lose control of the company.
     B: Yes, but if we <u>don't</u> agree to the deal, the company will <u>collapse</u>.
   b A: If we increase our prices, we will make more profit.
     B: Yes, but if we <u>decrease</u> our prices, we will get more <u>customers</u>.
   c A: If we move production to Asia, costs will go down.
     B: Yes, and if we <u>don't</u> move production to Asia, we will be <u>uncompetitive</u>.

Unit 10

Get ready to listen and speak
◉ b 5 c 3 d 6 e 1 f 4 g 7

A

1 b chequebook c balance d current account e abroad
  f savings account g bill h traveller's cheques i overdraft
  j bank card
2 2 j 3 f 4 g
3 2 Replacement OK. Need to telephone 24-hr emergency number.
  3 Need paying-in slip + bank card. Regular Saver or Bonus Saver account?
  4 OK but takes seven working days.

Focus on money

b lend money to someone c withdraw money from your account
d deposit a cheque into your account e arrange an overdraft

b in c out d in / out e for f in

B

1 e-Savings

2

Type of savings account	Interest rate	When interest is paid	Conditions
First reserve	**3.5%**	annually	at least **$5,000**
Bonus Saver	3%	every three months	**30** days' notice before withdrawal
Regular Saver	2.3%	**every month**	no interest paid if withdraw money
e-Savings	**4.1%**	every month	save at least **$75** per month

C

1 <u>Does that mean</u> I can get at the money immediately?
3 Your own answers. Possible answers:
  b Do you mean that I can't withdraw the money for three years?
  c So you're saying that I have to pay €295 if I want this account?
  d So that means the best rates you have are all online?
  e Do you mean that the interest rate won't go up or down?

D

1 <u>What do you mean by</u> 'penalty'?
3 Your own answers. Possible answers:
  b What do you mean by 'secured'?
  c What do you mean by 'minimum balance'?
  d What exactly does 'lump sum' mean?
  e Can you explain what 'automatic fee-free overdraft' means, please?

Focus on conditionals

b you take / you won't get c unless you have d you open / you will get e you aren't

E

1 a top up your mobile phone b apply for a driving licence
  c pay utility bills d exchange currency e redirect post
  f collect their pension g transfer money h buy phone cards
2 b A colleague. c Because she's posting the items outside the EU (Switzerland). d She decides to use the Airsure service.

Sound smart

2 a A: So I have to fill in a CN22 Customs label?
     B: No, you need to fill in a CN<u>23</u> Customs label.
   b A: So I fill in a VN1 form and then go to the Payment section?
     B: No, go to the <u>Payment section first</u> and <u>then</u> you can fill in a VN1.
   c A: Did you say it will take two weeks by standard mail?
     B: No, it'll take <u>three</u> weeks by standard mail. It'll take <u>two</u> weeks if you send it <u>Swiftmail</u>.

3

		CUSTOMS DECLARATION DÉCLARATION EN DOUANE		**CN 22** May be opened officially Peut être ouvert d'office

Great Britain\Grande-Bretagne   **Important! See instructions on the back**

	Gift\Cadeau		✓	Commercial sample\Echantillon commercial
	Documents			Other\Autre *Tick one or more boxes*

Quantity and detailed description of contents (1) Quantité et description détaillée du contenu	Weight (*in kg*)(2) Poids	Value (3) Valeur
Brochures		£10
DVD (x10)		£30

For commercial items only If known, HS tariff number (4) and country of origin of goods (5) N°tarifaire du SH et pays d'origine des marchandises (si connus)	Total Weight Poids total (*in kg*) (6)	Total Value (7) Valeur totale
HS238 UK	1.3	£40

I, the undersigned, whose name and address are given on the item, certify that the particulars given in this declaration are correct and that this item does not contain any dangerous article or articles prohibited by legislation or by postal or customs regulations

Date and sender's signature (8)   *Birgitte Tenkhoff   July 3rd '20*

4
b £5.28   c three days   d £5.89   e £9.39   f two days   g £10.09

Unit 11

Get ready to listen and speak

◉ *Your own answers.*
◉ police: car, station, siren, force
    fire: brigade, fighter, alarm, engine, station
◉ b witness   c commit   d break   e catch   f investigate
    g escape   h arrest   i charge

A

2 b 12.30pm   c theft   d outside the library   e Wen Ling Tsai
    f 17a Park Avenue, Bristol BR2 6YT   g Bag stolen   h Male.
    Medium height, short dark hair, glasses, moustache. Wearing blue
    jeans, black jumper, white running shoes.   i Bag is small, black,
    made of leather. Zip along top, shoulder strap, small tear on handle.

Focus on adjectives to describe appearance

Height / build: stocky, slim, muscular, skinny, overweight
Hair: straight, wavy, permed, curly, shoulder-length
Age: forty-ish
Face: oval, round, square
Style of dress: casual, scruffy, smart

B

1 He was <u>medium height</u> with <u>short dark hair</u> and <u>glasses</u>. Oh, and he
    had a <u>moustache</u>.
2 *Your own answers. Possible answers*:
    a He's short and stocky with long wavy dark hair and a square face.
        He's wearing some white tracksuit bottoms and a blue top. He
        looks in his early 20s and he's quite scruffy.
    b He's tall, possibly in his 50s, with short grey hair. He's slightly
        overweight, and has a round face. He's wearing a blue jacket and
        a patterned tie, with white trousers and black shoes. He looks very
        smart.

    c She's tall, rather skinny and she looks in her 30s. She has long
        straight red hair and an oval face. She looks very smart. She's
        wearing a black skirt and matching jacket. She's got some black
        high heels on and she's carrying a briefcase.
    d He's medium height, possibly in his mid-20s, and has short blond
        hair and a moustache. He's wearing dark glasses, a pair of blue
        jeans and a black jumper. He's got on a pair of white running
        shoes. He looks fairly casual.
    e She's short and she looks in her 20s. She's got shoulder-length,
        permed black hair and an oval face. She's wearing a blue and
        white striped dress and has a red coat with scarf and hat. She's got
        brown shoes.

C

1 It's a <u>small, black leather</u> bag, with a <u>zip along the top</u> and a <u>shoulder
    strap</u>.
2 *Your own answers. Possible answers*:
    b It's a medium-sized red handbag with a flap over the front and a
        shoulder strap.
    c It's a large-ish multicoloured cloth bag with two handles. It doesn't
        have a zip or catch.
    d It's a small overnight bag. It's black and looks quite square. It has
        two handles.
    e It's a large green suitcase, possibly made of plastic, with a white
        ribbon tied around, probably to help identify it. It has an airmail tag
        on one handle. The other handle is extendable. It also has wheels.

Focus on order of adjectives

b new black denim   c wonderful pink diamond
d large rectangular mahogany   e tall French crystal

D

1 c
2 Where do you need the ambulance to come to?   2
    Which service do you require?   1
    What's happened?   3
    How many people are hurt?   4

3 1 Ambulance.   2 Green Park.
    3 There's been a traffic accident. A car has hit a cyclist.
    4 Two (the car driver and the cyclist).

E

2 *Your own answers. Possible answers*:
    a Ambulance, please. / Richmond bus station. / An old woman
        has just fallen down. I think she's fainted. / Just her. She's on the
        ground. She isn't moving.
    b Fire service, please. / (*Your name*) / Outside Highcroft School. /
        In the school, upstairs. / I don't know. Maybe, but I can't see
        from here.

F

1 C
2 b True   c True   d False   e True   f False

Sound smart – The schwa

2 a How fast w<u>a</u>s the car trav<u>e</u>lling?
    b So th<u>e</u> c<u>o</u>llision happ<u>e</u>ned here, you say?
    c There w<u>a</u>s <u>a</u> big crash and then sil<u>e</u>nce.

Unit 12

○ b 4 c 6 d 1 e 2 f 5

A

1 Change some arrangements

2 *Your own answers. Possible answers*:

   b 0207-772994 (office)

   c Meet in his office in Building 3 (not the main building) at 4pm (not 2pm). Call before 1.30pm to confirm.

B

3 *Your own answers. Possible answers*:

   b Right. I think I've got that. You want to know if she has the blue file with this month's sales figures. You need it urgently.

   c Let me repeat that, just to make sure. She needs to complete her expense form and send it to you in Accounts by Friday lunchtime.

   d I'll just go over that to confirm. Her flight leaves at 3.30 and a taxi will pick her up outside her apartment at midday. Mr Wilkinson will meet her at the airport in Paris.

   e Let me repeat that, just to make sure. The price is $1,500, including delivery and installation, and you need an answer before eleven tomorrow.

Focus on telephoning

b hold c call d put e give f hear g get

2 e 3 d 4 a 5 b

C

2 Did you say …? Sorry. What was that last part again, please?

3 *Your own answers. Possible answers*:

   b You said Extension 349, right? c Did you say in the Baker Suite?

   d You said TX743, right? e Sorry. What was that last part again, please?

D

Your own answers. Possible answers:

b the marketing strategy report c valued customers d ordered from the company e average age f last summer's TV campaign g net income h the cost

E

1 b appreciate it c make sense d take a message e who's calling f got that g Who is this h Would you mind i appreciate your help j get your name k repeat that back

2 to ask to leave a message: d, h

   to thank the person taking the message: b, i,

   to check the person has understood you correctly: c, f, k

3 e, g, j

4 c, f, h, j

F

1 3 – 2 – 5 – 4 – 1

2 *Your own answers. Possible answers*:

   2 Give the reason for your call:

     I'm phoning to let you know that … / I'm calling to ask about …

   3 Say what action is necessary:

     Please phone me back. / Could you email me the report, please?

   4 Give your contact details, if necessary:

     You can call me on … / My email address is …

   5 Finish the call:

     Thanks a lot. Bye

3 *Your own answer. Possible answer*:

This is Sam Kershaw from Industrial Design. I'm phoning to let you know that your order is ready. You need to pay in full before we can send it to you. Please call Accounts to pay. You can ring me if necessary on my office number 0208-451-5690 or on my mobile 07969-431094. Thanks a lot. Bye.

Sound smart

2 b 8 c 10 d 12 e 12

Unit 13

○ b not present c private d suspend e achieve

○ b chair c agenda d minutes e compulsory f motion g objectives h show

A

1 b Do you see? c Could you say what you mean? d Let's move on, shall we? e It's a deal. f Yes, I agree.

2 b 6 c 10 d 8 e 8 f 6 g 8 h 6

3 b That's not right at all. c I think we're drifting off the point a bit. d Right, now let's move on, shall we? e Can you explain what you mean by that? f Could I come in here, please? g Let's get down to business, shall we? h What's your opinion on this?

5 1 g 2 h 4 d 5 c 6 e 7 b 8 f

6 How do you feel about …? 2 Right. Let's kick off with … 1 Sorry, but I don't agree. 7 I'm not sure that's relevant. 5 OK. Let's go on to … 4 What exactly do you mean? 6 Can I say something at this point? 8

B

1 We might consider …ing, I propose we …

2

Suggestions	Catherine	Mark	Julie	Peter
Spend more money on marketing	✗	✓	✓	✗
Hire a new sales manager	✓	✓	✓	✗

C

2 a I'd like to start by asking (name).

    (Name), do you have any thoughts?

    Perhaps you can give us your opinion, (name)?

    How do you feel about that, (name)?

    (Name)?

   b The chair is Catherine.

3 *Your own answers. Possible answers*:

   b Frances, do you have any thoughts?

   c How do you feel about that, Mr Gonzales?

   d Martha, what's your reaction?

   e Perhaps you could give us your opinion, Mrs Marsh?

D

1 I'm not very keen on that idea (at all). Reject

   I don't see it like that at all. Reject

   I couldn't disagree more. Reject

   I think that's a good idea. Accept

   I'm afraid that's not how I see it. Reject

   I have no problem with that. Accept

   That sounds reasonable to me. Accept

2 I think that's a good idea. I couldn't disagree more. That sounds reasonable to me. I have no problem with that. I'm afraid that's not how I see it. I'm not very keen on that idea at all.

3 *Your own answers. Possible answers:*
  b I have no problem with that.   c I'm not very keen on that idea.
  d I think that's a good idea.   e I couldn't disagree more.
  f That sounds reasonable to me.

Sound smart

2 The intonation goes up at the end of these sentences: b, e, f, h
  The intonation goes down at the end of these sentences: c, d, g

---

E

2 *Your own answers. Possible answers:*
  b Sorry. I think you've misunderstood me. I actually believe output
    will stay the same.
  c That's not quite what I meant. I meant we shouldn't launch later
    than February.
  d I don't think you understand what I mean. I'm saying that the
    investment could have been better.
  e Sorry. What I meant was I need time to think about it.

F

1 a ten percent bonus / double within six months
  b a success / reliability and pricing
  c staff redundancies / spring
2 a just summarize the main points.
  b go over today's main points.
  c sum up, then …
3 I think we've covered everything, so shall we call it a day? It looks like we
  can finish early today. We'll have to cut this meeting short, I'm afraid.

Unit 14

Get ready to listen and speak

  b 3 c 1 d 4
  Your own answer.
  Your own answers.

A

Extract 1: c   Extract 2: b   Extract 3: b

B

2 animals, transport, the weather, food, carbon dioxide, recycling
3 a
4 b
5 Consequences   2
  What governments should do   4
  Statistics   1
  What we can do   3
  Fight for survival   5

Focus on signposts

Moreover c   In addition c   For example b
To illustrate this b   This is why … a   Therefore a   Also c

---

C

2 Jorge's notes are better. They are more concise, and easier to follow
  as he numbers the key points. He uses abbreviations and symbols to
  reduce the number of words. He covers all key points.
  Cynthia's notes could be more concise (the phrases are too long). She
  doesn't number any points, or use abbreviations or symbols.

---

2 *Your own answers. Possible answers:*
  <u>What we can do</u>
  1 Recycling
    Recycle everything
    Buy recycled goods
  2 Food
    Buy fresh food (frozen uses 10x more energy)
    Locally grown food
  3 Save energy
    Save 30% if turn off lights / use long-life bulbs (60% more eff)
    Use a/c less
    Wash clothes at a lower temp.
    X use d-washer
    OFF appliances when not using
  4 Transport
    X car >> public transport / walk / cycle
    Car pool / check tyres (3% more eff)

Sound smart

2   more slowly   louder   pausing

	more slowly	louder	pausing
a		✓	
b			✓
c	✓		
d			✓
e	✓		

3 Yes, there are <u>many</u> things you can do. And there are many things
  the <u>government</u> can do too. Did you know there are over <u>200</u>
  <u>separate environmental agreements</u>? Sounds impressive, doesn't
  it? Until you realize all of them are hard to <u>enforce</u> and <u>poorly</u>
  coordinated. Each government needs to pass effective laws to <u>force</u>
  individuals <u>and</u> industry to take <u>responsibility</u> for climate change.

D

1 Something I didn't agree with was   c
  Basically, it was about   a
  They said / claimed / argued that   b
  There were three main points.   b
2 *Your own answer. Possible answer:*
  Basically, it was about global warming. She gave lots of examples to
  show how global warming would affect the planet in the future. She also
  suggested things we can all do to stop the situation getting worse, like
  recycling and saving energy. I think that was the most interesting part.

Unit 15

Get ready to listen and speak

  b 3 c 1 d 7 e 10 f 4 g 8 h 9 i 5 j 2
  Audience – who you are speaking to
  Content – what you want to say
  Organization – how you want to structure your talk
  Venue – where you will be giving the talk
  Time – how long you have
  Your own answers.

A

1 introduce the subject   2
  give an overview of the structure of the talk   3
  explain rules for questions   4
2 b going to talk   c start by   d Then I'll   e After that   f finally, I'll
  g have time for

Answer key

B

1 a Welcoming your audience:
Good morning to you all.
Hello. Thank you for giving me this opportunity to …

    b Introducing your subject:
Today I want to talk to you about …

    c Giving an overview of your talk:
First of all, I'll go over some background details.
To start with, I'll review …
I'll start by describing …
Then I'll look at …
After that, I'll move on to …
Finally, I'll review the main points.

    d Explaining rules for questions:
Feel free to interrupt me if you have any questions.
I'll make sure we have enough time for questions at the end.

2 *Your own answers. Possible answers:*
First of all, I'll explain where we are now. Then I'll look at our restructuring plans. After that, I'll move on to our expansion into Asia. And finally, I'll review our long-term goals. If you have any questions, please feel free to ask me any time.

C

1 <u>Finishing one point</u>
all I have to say
<u>Starting another point</u>
like to turn to
<u>Giving an example</u>
give you an

2 <u>Finishing one point</u>
I've told you about our pensions policy.
<u>Starting another point</u>
Let me now turn to staff recruitment.
<u>Giving an example</u>
A good example of this is …

Sound smart

2 Speaker 2

3 Speaker 1 is too slow and his voice is too low. His voice also drops at the end of sentences, making it difficult to hear. He fails to emphasize important points.
Speaker 2 has a clear delivery and varies her voice well to emphasize important points. She also pauses between points to engage the interest and attention of the audience.
Speaker 3 speaks too quickly, making it hard for the audience to follow. She does not pause at the relevant points, but pauses at inappropriate points simply to draw breath.

D

1 thanks the audience   2
summarizes the main points   1
invites questions   3

2 a sum up b review c conclusion d you all for e much for your f have any questions g Can I answer h any final

4 To sum up briefly, then …
Thank you all for listening.
Now, does anyone have any quesions?

E

Sure. Go ahead.
Yes? Please ask your question.
Yes, of course. What would you like to know?
Now, does anyone else have a question?

F

2 *Your own answers. Possible answers:*
    b There's no time now, but let's chat about it afterwards.
    c I'm not quite sure I agree with you on that.
    d That's a very good point. What does everyone else think?
    e There's no time now, but let's chat about it afterwards.

G

1 *Your own answers.*

Unit 16

Get ready to listen and speak

- In a seminar:
you are free to express your views.
The purpose of a seminar is:
to encourage open debate.
to help students learn from each other.
to explore a topic in more detail.
- F F F

A

1 He covers points 1, 2 and 4, but not point 3 fully.

2 The topic is Learning styles.

3
Learning style	Advice for studying
Visual	use charts and pictures, colour highlighting
Auditory	read aloud, listen
Reading	read
Kinaesthetic	revise standing up, move around

4 *Your own answers. Possible answers:*
a No (Not really stated.) b No (No handouts, can't remember key name, can't pronounce key word.) c Yes (At least, the beginning is clear.) d No e Yes (Fairly easy to follow.) f No (He sounds nervous.)

5 The talk is OK so far. It seems clearly organized, although it has some flaws (see above).

B

1 b No c No d Yes e No

2 c

Sound smart

2 Speaker 1 sounds more enthusiastic. She speaks in a higher pitch than normal, clearly emphasizes the key words, makes her voice go up and down to maintain the audience's interest, and sounds enthusiastic.

C

2 In other words, …, The point I'm making is …

3 *Your own answers. Possible answers:*
    b The point I'm making is that we don't know the exact process by which we 'learn' something.
    c In other words, we don't know which learning style is best.

D

1 *Your own answers.*

3 Answers:
Advantages of being multimodal?
Flexibility, can learn in many situations
Is VARK a learning style?
Yes (informs how we learn)

Are learning styles fixed?
Basics, yes (don't stop being a visual learner) but develop too
Men–women differences?
No

4 *Your own answer. Possible answer*:
Greg answers the questions better once students have reworded their questions.

E

2 That's not really what I was asking. I meant … I think you've answered a slightly different question. What I want to know is …

3 *Your own answers. Possible answers*:
  b Perhaps my question wasn't very clear. Actually, I was asking you to say what the value is of studying learning styles.
  c That's not really what I was asking. I meant, if we study all the learning styles, will we become better learners?

Review 2

1 1 a, 2 a, 3 b, 4 b, 5 c, 6 a, 7 b, 8 c, 9 b, 10 c
2 1 a, 2 a, 3 c, 4 c, 5 a, 6 b, 7 b, 8 a, 9 c, 10 a
3 1 b, 2 b, 3 c, 4 c, 5 b, 6 b, 7 a, 8 b, 9 c, 10 a
4 *Your own answers. Possible answers*:
  1 No, not at all. / Fine. That's OK with me.
  2 You can't expect me to wait that long. / I'm sorry, but that's no good at all. / I really must insist that you do something sooner. / Is that the best you can do?
  3 He had medium-length fair hair with a beard and glasses. He was quite scruffy, and he was wearing blue jeans and a white jacket.
  4 Sorry, I don't understand. What does 'putting the cart before the horse' mean?
  5 Is that your best offer? / You'll have to do better than that, I'm afraid.
  6 Yes, of course. First of all I'll … , then I'll look at … and after that I'll move on to … Finally I'll …
  7 Any time after six. / Sometime between one and two would be good. / Shall we say eleven o'clock? / How about four thirty?
  8 Yes, I do. / No, that's not quite what I meant. I think you've misunderstood me. / I'm afraid you haven't understood what I'm getting at.
  9 It was a black leather bag, quite large, with a long shoulder strap and a zip along the top.
  10 Hello. It's Stephan. I'm calling about the contract for the new equipment. We have just sent it today. Please can you let me know when you receive it? You can call me on 4875601. Many thanks.